DIARY OF A LOLLIPOP IN A PEANUT FACTORY

BY

JANE ELISSA

Decadent Publishing Company
www.decadentpublishing.com

Diary of a Lollipop in a Peanut Factory
Copyright 2012 by Jane Elissa
ISBN: 978-1-61333-361-7
Cover design by Greg Hallam based on a Jane Elissa Design
Photographs by Sue Coflin/Max Photos

Published by Decadent Publishing Company, LLC
Look for us online at:
www.decadentpublishing.com

Printed in the United States of America

Jane Elissa will donate a portion of her profits from Diary of a Lollipop in a Peanut Factory to charity.

~Foreword~

*K*udos to fashion designer and charity impresario Jane Elissa. She's written a poignant biography of love, loss, and the struggle for self-expression. Her book includes a celebrity collection of remembrances set in the heart of New York's theatrical district when fan fever defined the final years of Soap Opera Madness and Broadway Spectacles.

Jane's recall of famous friendships takes readers on a trip down memory lane and highlights how the stars of stage and TV screens befriended and supported her fashions, art work, and fundraisers.

Her efforts to help leukemia research are legendary. She started small but grew her fashion shows into highly successful Manhattan extravaganzas. Jane attracted enthusiastic celebrities and introduced innovative ideas for raffles and auctions, which stand as a blueprint for anyone interested in creating successful charitable events today.

Diary of a Lollipop in a Peanut Factory follows Jane's growth as an artist in search of identity and a woman in need of emotional help and personal happiness. She describes her emergence from tragedy and how she faces the future with her skills and achievements intact. Jane Elissa was blessed with a survivor gene and sparkling charisma.

As an artist specializing in exalting Broadway and Times

Square in collage formats on all mediums, Jane ran her *atelier* and set up shop in the heart of the theater district on Broadway. She socialized early on with Broadway luminaries who passed through the Great White Way when Times Square stood in the center of the universe.

The stars of stage and screen (TV that is) were attracted to Jane's artistic rendering of Broadway, her original clothing designs, and her flamboyant personality—and vice-versa. She loved performers and was the biggest Broadway fan. Not only did actresses revel in wearing her creations and making her name well known, but they invited co-stars to appear with them at fashion shows raising hundreds of thousands of dollars for leukemia research. Jane's mother, who was plagued by the disease, was the inspiration for her daughter's passion to organize an annual charitable event.

How Jane morphed into a Broadway designer/charity fundraiser *extraordinaire* is a heroic New York story that only she could live to tell. Along with winning people skills and original creative ideas, like all great achievers, Jane has unflagging energy, vision, and relies on her inner muse. She is intuitively open to artistic opportunities even in the face of great personal setbacks or economic crisis; "always keeping her eye on the ball," to quote a New York expression.

The cast of famous characters in her biography include soap opera actors from long running series. But like old soldiers who fade away, many familiar characters have retired and are rarely heard from today. Readers can wax nostalgic over some of Jane's encounters and remember the good old days.

On the other hand, her contacts include many of today's hot shots of film and television who cut their teeth on soaps and the Broadway stage. How she relishes visiting them on trips to L.A.

Jane's journey and photographs may raise your hopes that the soaps could replace tedious reality shows and real acting talents could once again reign over afternoon television. But don't lose sleep over that fantasy! Everything changes, nothing stays the same. Except for Jane!

She was familiar with some of the great performers of Broadway's classic musicals. What a treat it was to attend her events and hear awesome Broadway voices—the lead performers from *Jekyll and Hyde, Phantom of the Opera,* and *Les Miz,* including my favorite, golden-voiced Bob Evans.

As a designer, Jane's unique New York City art work appears on all her creations—jackets, purses, capes, caps, and hats, paintings, posters, souvenir glasses, and mugs. Her work is sold through trunk shows, fashion fairs, RT Booklovers Convention, online sites, and other public venues.

She still delights fashionistas of all ages with her one-of-a kind designs and her sales pitch is memorable. No one tries a hat on your head or drapes a shawl on your shoulders with such panache as Jane Elissa.

She is timeless and treasured for her Broadway collages on fashionable, wearable art. If George M. Cohan could see her now!

As I write this, I'm happy to announce that my husband, who was diagnosed with hairy-cell leukemia, is in remission, thanks to the remarkable Leukemia Foundation. In addition to feeling grateful, I'm drinking my coffee out of a Jane Elissa black ceramic mug, adorned with a familiar scene of Times Square ablaze with lights. Racing yellow taxis and theater goers scurry along Broadway under the marquees of glittering productions ready for opening night. May Broadway live forever.

I thank Jane for her contribution to preserving Times Square and New York through her art. And I commend her for inspiring so many performers and fans to support leukemia research.

She is a living symbol of the Big Apple and deserves a Big Heart that says "I love Jane Elissa."

August, 2012
Kathryn Falk, Lady of Barrow
Founder of RT Book Reviews Magazine

~Author's Note~

. . . *H*ave you ever felt "out of place," miscast, lost, alone, not
fitting in?
Well, that has always been me....

"The lollipop in the peanut factory"
where everyone else is strong with a hard shell,
looking the same, working together
to produce more peanuts—
and I, the lollipop,
standing aside becoming soft and mushy
and eventually fading away,
but never being part of the group....

This is my story of learning to accept myself.

For all who need to find their place...
Enjoy

The Unexpected

1987

...*M*onday morning, three flights up, sewing machines whirring, scissors cutting, fabric laced across the floor, television humming.

It began with a phone call.

"Leukemia Society."

"Hi, my name is Jane Elissa, and I just glimpsed your promo on *Regis and Kathy Lee*. I'd like to speak to someone in charge of the Mets' Wives' fashion show."

"Are you calling to buy a ticket?"

"No."

"Just a minute, please."

After what seemed like an interminable amount of time, someone new came on. "Leukemia Society."

Again, "My name is Jane Elissa—"

A ringing phone in the background. "Hold a minute, please."

Again, waiting.... Finally, a new woman came on the phone. "How can I help you?"

"I'm calling because I saw your Mets' Wives' fashion show advertised—"

"Where did you see it?"

"On *Regis and Kathy Lee*," I replied.

"How did you get this number?"

"It flashed across the bottom of the screen."

"And you're calling to buy tickets?"

"No." I was practically shouting now. "I'm a designer. My mother was recently diagnosed with leukemia. I would like to donate a handmade shawl to your Mets' Wives' luncheon."

"Sorry—the designer is bringing all the clothes."

"Perhaps I could volunteer to help dress the models backstage," I said.

"Not necessary. The designer is bringing everyone. You can buy a ticket."

"I don't want to buy a ticket."

Click.

I sat there stunned. They didn't want my help? They didn't ask about my mom's leukemia? They were not very responsive. Who were these people? I called again.

"Leukemia Society."

"I'm calling because I'm also a designer, and I'd like to put on a fashion show of my own."

Where did that come from?

"I'll have to have someone call you back. Name and phone number, please. Thank you. Good-bye." *Click.*

First Year

Now what do I do? Someone will call me—when? In three years? Mom had just been diagnosed with CLL, a form of leukemia that is chronic, which means, although it has to be monitored, it is a long term disease. I did not know that at the time, and I was anxious to do something immediately. I needed information about the disease if I were going to do something useful. Blood cancer and often fatal—that's all I knew.

Anne Levack from the Leukemia Society called me that week. She sounded friendly, appreciative of my phone call, and she offered to help. We made plans to get together at my studio the following week. We had to be "presentable." The studio would have to be swept—no scraps on the floor, threads on my dress, or pins sticking out of my jacket. Usually my studio whirled with activity—phones ringing; fabric being measured, cut, and appliquéd on garments; large rolls of silk piled against the walls, shawls pinned to the brick walls, and racks full of T-shirts. Now, we would have to be neat and appear organized to impress Anne.

When she arrived, she immediately struck me as a serious person. She was cordial but focused as she outlined the goals of the LLS. One of the things Anne stressed was that they were always looking for ways to raise money, but they also *did not do* any of the preparation for an event. They would assign someone to help me from their office, but they were not responsible for selling tickets or promotion. Each event had to be self-contained, which meant that I had to provide everything—venue, invitations, staff, favors, models, clothes, etc.

How do I do that?

တ

As a young girl I had studied both piano and singing, and at that time, I was renewing my love for singing by taking what I called "fun" lessons. I had found a teacher who specialized in people like me, people who had abandoned stretching their vocal cords and just wanted to retrain the muscle so they could actually carry a tune again. It was embarrassing to me to hear my voice as it was then, and I wanted to at least enjoy singing karaoke. My teacher, Marty, had worked with Bob McGrath from *Sesame Street* and had emceed shows on cruise ships. He had a wonderful sense of humor. He also had some pupils who were more serious than I was and were appearing on Broadway at that time.

He promised to ask them if they would like to participate in my fashion show and to ask any other show biz people he knew. He also volunteered to be our host emcee, which was a great plus because of his experience and support for the cause.

"You can do this," he would say.

I just laughed. It was better than crying.

တ

I knew very little about fashion shows, but I did have beautiful clothing and accessories. Our designs were made by hand with vintage flowers, which we cut from old silk shawls I used to find at flea markets and thrift stores. I had part-time sewers that made the clothes, and we then painted and appliquéd them. The colors were vivid and the designs eye-catching. I quickly learned from listening to other designers that to present a good fashion show, the bolder and more unusual the designs, the more interested people would be.

I was not, however, really thinking about showing the clothes as much as I was concerned about getting people to attend. I also had no idea where to have the event. The coincidences of life always amaze me though. When you start on a path, even if you have no real plan in mind, things will fall into place. You have to have *the will* to push forward.

My friend Annie Santiago loved to dance. On the weekends, I would meet her at a disco in the NY Hilton Hotel named Pursuits. There, people could have dinner, dance and spend a quiet evening on a date, or have a drink at the bar with friends. It was not a typical New York disco because the people that frequented the club were often tourists from the hotel or older people from the tri-state area. The music was not loud and blaring, and although the entry fee was included, overall it was expensive for a club. The dress code included a sport jacket for men, and on the weekends, suits and ties. We became acquainted with a lot of the regulars who went there. Eventually, I met the club manager, who in time, began noticing my wardrobe (I often wore a "Jane Elissa" shawl, purse, or jacket.), and she frequently commented favorably on the items. We were talking one day, and I told her I wanted to put on a fashion show to benefit the LLS. We needed a space, but the budget did not include a room rental fee as this was the inaugural event. I was not even sure if we had an audience to come or if we would make any money.

She said, "I have the perfect solution for you. We have a happy hour and a complimentary buffet during the week. Why don't you have your fashion show during Secretaries' Week on that Wednesday, and you will have a built-in audience. We'll give out cards to the hotel guests and do a mailing to the businesses in the neighborhood. Anyone you invite will also be able to enjoy the drinks and buffet."

It sounded perfect! We agreed I would have a volunteer at the door to collect a small donation, and the dance floor would make a perfect stage. We would be able to use the small storage room off the dance floor as a dressing room, and they would provide a podium and microphone for the commentary and introductions. They also gave us coat racks to hold the clothes for the models and tables and chairs for backstage. All I had to do was choose the clothes, fit the models, *find* the models, write the show order, go over the commentary with Marty, etc., etc., etc.

I wanted the program to be fun. I could not put together a serious fashion show. Presenting a line with models is very different than staging an entertainment event. This show was just the vehicle to get people into the club to donate money and learn more about the cause. Anne Levack tried to reassure me. She just kept telling me, "Whatever you make is more than we had before." But I could not help being anxious.

At a professional fashion show, although it is enjoyable, the goal is to *sell* the apparel. The models, although beautiful, are really "hangers" for the designer's line. The clothes are the stars. The buyers then feature these wearables in their stores, magazines, TV shows, and so on. Our show did not have that same purpose. We wanted to present the model as the *star*, and the clothes were the means to entertain. Therefore, they had to be colorful, extravagant, sexy, different, and fun so that people could say they saw these celebrities having a good time. Eventually, I would learn more about fashion shows, but for that first one, the audience would be there to see the models.

Where would they come from? Anne said she would speak to a couple of her friends who knew some up-and-coming daytime television actors and actresses. Lucky for me, there were three that she found who were young and beautiful and willing to donate their time. She also posted a notice at some of the soaps that we were looking for volunteers. Marty brought a pupil who worked on an ABC soap and another student who was performing on Broadway. I dragged my gorgeous cousin Jill in to model along with her daughter Ingrid. We may have had a total of ten people, but they were all very supportive and eager to have fun, show the clothes, and help the charity. All of us were in a learning mode.

The models came to my studio loft apartment, and we fitted them with three or four different outfits. We were making colorful camisoles and silk teddies with velvet and silk kimonos for the boudoir. There were also painted tee shirts, embroidered shawls, and delicate lace Victorian blouses to present. We thought this array of day and evening wear would have enough variety to interest the audience.

Jensen Buchanan, who played Sarah on *One Life To Live*, was beautiful and easy to fit. Her friend, Lonnie Quinn, a new actor on *All My Children* was also accommodating and easy to work with. Jessica Tuck, Megan on *One Life To Live*, seemed a little shyer and more self-conscious so we worked the clothes around her concerns. Tamara Tunie, who appeared on *As The World Turns*, saw a notice Anne Levack had posted at her studio requesting models and volunteered. She had a fabulous model's body and knew how to strut the runway. We picked great colors for her and another actor Christopher Durham from *All My Children*. It was coming together, but we did not have a particular theme. I would develop that later.

We could not rehearse with the stars because they worked during the day, and at night when the club was open, we couldn't use the facilities. The show would have to be done "on the fly," a term I later learned. I would need to at least prepare a lineup with some continuity so that it made sense to the audience. I envisioned the models' progression starting with casual day wear, then on to business attire, and eventually into evening wear. I also included the bedtime wear because it was a little skimpier and gave the models an opportunity to entice the audience and be more playful. I did not really know how to direct the models in their presentation, but I did make suggestions. They were actors, so if I used the words "flirt with the audience," they knew what to do.

We arrived in two taxis at Pursuits the afternoon of the show and had no idea how many people were coming. Anne had some people from the LLS there to help us in the changing room, and I brought some volunteer friends. The club manager said she'd had a positive response from the hotel guests, so we anticipated about fifty to seventy-five people would attend. The enticement of free drinks, food, and fashion would certainly be enough to draw in a crowd—I hoped.

The staff at the hotel accommodated us by bringing in food, cold drinks for the models and volunteers, and even gave us one or two people to help backstage. To say I was nervous would be an understatement. I was petrified. I did not even want to look out from behind the curtain to see the audience. I did know that some of the people I socialized with on the weekends might be there, but I did not really want to see anyone. I had so many doubts. What if someone fell? What if only ten people attended? What if no one applauded at the clothes? What if, what if...?

So many people buzzing around—clothes all labeled with models' names, people ready to provide the next outfit when they came back after each turn, safety pins to hold straps up, needle and thread for rips, bobby pins for hair, sparkling jewelry to accessorize, Marty's line-up, timing—not too long, no more than forty-five minutes. Would he be able to fill in if we were late? Would there be applause?

"Don't worry"—came Marty's booming voice—"it will be fine."

Intro music—quiet in the back—Marty was welcoming everyone. It had begun.

I never peeked out to see the crowd. From the other side of the curtain, I did hear laughter and applause. Marty called and introduced the models. The disco played quiet music. Everyone was smiling while the butterflies danced in my stomach. In and out, clothes dropped on the floor. New outfits, make sure it fits right, long jacket, kimono, teddy....

And then it was over. "Take a bow, Jane," someone called.

I took two of my helpers with me. I was *so* shy I wore sunglasses so I did not have to see people. I did glimpse my mom, friend Ilene Butler and my brother Joel—but no one else. Everything blurred....

Breathe.

Hugs for everyone—Marty had done a fabulous job. He kept the flow of the show moving, and I thanked him over and over. The models thanked me, and Jensen told me to come and sell products in the *One Life To Live* dressing area for Christmas. I said, "sure" and offered everyone a Jane Elissa item for themselves. They refused insisting everything should be for charity, and they might buy things from us in the future. They were extremely gracious but left very quickly as they had to be on set early the next day. I gave the club manager a scarf and thanked her, and Anne Levack was smiling and telling me what an enjoyable time everyone had.

Breathe again.

People wanted to say hello, so I had to go out and greet them. One of my male friends from the weekends gave me a big hug and said, "Your first professional show and you tried it out on us 'lounge lizards.' Good job. Thanks."

I laughed. A bunch of people I did not know came up to me. "Thank you for coming. Hope you enjoyed it."

"We had a great time."

"Do it again."

"Good Luck with your charity work."

Over and over again—this was good.

Finally, I saw my family and friends. I sat down for a quick ginger ale, and I told Ilene to tell me the next day what needed to be fixed. After all, this was only our first attempt, and I was sure there were many *faux pas*. If I had to do another one, I needed constructive criticism, and I needed Ilene to tell me the truth.

While we were packing everything to return to my studio loft, a few people came back into the room to meet me. One of them was Rita Salk, a publicist who had approached Anne about helping us recruit volunteer soap actors and actresses for the fashion show. She said many of her clients would be interested in helping out. Rita was a gray-haired, fast-talking, jovial woman from the South. She was as lively as I was quiet, and she sparkled when she spoke.

Rita puttered around backstage looking at all the clothes. "Did you make all these?" she asked.

"Yes," Avé, my fellow designer, answered.

"Well, I'll be..." was all I remember her saying, and she kept poking through the racks as the volunteers were trying to pack. Eventually, she whirled around and shook her finger at me. "My dear," she said, "you need a publicist. You should be *everywhere!*"

I smiled. "Right now I'd like to be in bed with my feet up and my eyes closed."

"We have to talk. Here's my card. Call me...."

That was the start of a lifelong relationship with a woman who would become not only a huge asset to my charity work but also a dear friend.

I met another person that night, one who would become my *compadre* in life, Annie Albarian. She introduced herself and told me about her love of soaps and that she wanted to volunteer to help out with the shows. A tall, beautiful redhead with intense hazel eyes, she wore an exquisite designer suit. Annie had come to New York from Lebanon to study medicine. Her appreciation of daytime dramas had started early in her life, and she enjoyed meeting some of the actors. She gave me her card and told me to keep in touch with her as she would love to work on the fashion show. Her medical school commitment, however, limited her free time, but whenever she could, she would be excited to help. If not, she promised to come to the next one and bring friends. I knew I liked her and would be in touch.

I do not even remember how we got everything back that night, but I do know I did *not* work the next day. I just wanted a break.

After the First Year

I was so grateful to be finished with my first fashion show that I didn't think further. What did I need to know? We raised seven hundred dollars, but it probably cost me tons more with my time and expenses. Yet, we were meeting celebrities and going to the studios—who could resist?

Anne Levack, from the Leukemia Lymphoma Society, suggested we do another event the following year. Rita Salk wanted to help, and I agreed to try another fashion show.

The next two years were building years although I didn't know it at the time. My art-to-wear business was growing, and we were making many different kinds of clothing. Stores were selling our Victorian designed blouses, jackets, and velvet cocoons and kimonos. I was taking more chances in my designs, and people seemed to like the new direction. We were making private label lace items for Shell Kepler, who at the time played Amy Vining on *General Hospital*.

And that brings me to another story....

ప్ర

Before I even started the fashion shows, I loved watching the daytime drama *General Hospital*. Mom had watched all the soaps, as they were known on ABC, and it was a bonding experience to come home from school, have an afternoon snack, and watch them with her. One of the actresses on *General Hospital* was Finola Hughes. We thought she was so classy and beautiful. I wanted to be like her. Avé and I took to wearing our hair with a "poof" as we called it, just like Finola. We grabbed a bit of hair on top of our heads and pushed it back to be held down with a clip. We thought we were *so cool*. Truthfully, people did tell me I resembled her, and it thrilled me to be like my "idol."

One afternoon, my mom called me and told me she saw that Finola would be coming to New York to meet her fans with some other soap opera stars including James Mitchell from *All My Children*, John Loprino from *One Life To Live*, and Ian Buchanan from *General Hospital*. Mom wanted to go to this "fan fest" so I bought tickets. It was held at the Milford Plaza Hotel. While Finola was signing autographs, I gave her a shawl I had made, and she couldn't have been more gracious. Mom told her about all the things I designed, and Finola said she would like to come to see my items. I almost fainted.

The next morning around ten, she called me and subwayed down to visit at my place. At that time, I lived in a carriage house, a mini-house the size of a cottage from the 1800s, on 23rd Street, which I shared with a friend. We worked there as well. It was located behind a larger apartment building and to get in, people had to ring the bell to open the gate, and then travel through the very dark and narrow walkway on the side until they saw the cute little place. It was a rare piece of Manhattan real estate. I found it because I had become friends with the owner and he needed to rent it, so I took it.

There were three floors. I worked there, slept upstairs, and had my own bathroom. The first night there I discovered something called "roof rats," and I heard mice squeak as they raced through the walls. Never mind the roaches and water bugs. Needless to say, in one week I had two exterminators, a total overhaul on the floors, a new paint job, and *Brillo* in the bricks. It was to this lovely place that Finola came.

We sat in my bedroom and tiny workroom while she tried on

clothes. She was absolutely charming and fun. We talked about New York as she did not know much about the city. She also wanted to know about my mom. I had asked my mom to come as she was staying Uptown with my brother, but for some reason she said no. That struck me as very odd since my mother is the ultimate "groupie." She loved show business and celebrities, but that time she let me be alone. I took this as a gift because I never could have spoken so openly with Finola if my mom had been there.

Finola ended up buying two beautiful silk Victorian blouses. We talked about many things, and I remember her saying how nice it would be to have a child, "a little friend" as she called it. Then my roommate Johanna came home. I introduced them, and Jo reminded me that we had theater tickets and it was getting late. Finola had to leave anyway, so I gave her directions back to the subway and to her next destination. That time with her will always be very special to me, and I have only the fondest memories of her.

We were unable to meet up again because of her busy schedule, so sadly, our connection never grew. But from that short time, I have a lifetime memory.

Ernie

...When the unexpected happens it feels like magic...

You walk into a restaurant on a Friday night. The lights are dim, the music is mellow, and the conversation is casual. You are with a friend—sharing your daily woes, occasionally having a laugh about the mishaps of the week. You look around at the other people eating and wonder what their lives are like. Your eyes wander. Your friend goes to the ladies' room. You have a sip of your tea.... A couple nearby is laughing and holding hands. He puts his arm on her shoulder and she leans against him. You sense a warmth between them, and it reminds you that you are alone....

And then you see him.

He is standing with another man, talking animatedly by the bar. He is tall, dark-skinned with broad shoulders. He is wearing a black sports jacket and black pants with a cream-colored shirt. For a moment you think he sees you, but then he continues talking to his companion so you think not. Your imagination takes over—

What do I do now? I want to meet him.... Do I walk by? Do I smile? Do I just finish my tea and go home?

"Jane...are you all right? You seem to be off somewhere else." Annie Santiago's voice interrupted my musings.

"Sorry. I was planning my day for tomorrow." I lied to her. I did not want to tell her I was thinking about a stranger and his friend at the bar.

"Well," she said, "just to let you know, I met a friend of mine coming back from the ladies' room and he wants to join us for dessert. Is that okay?"

"Sure," I said automatically. "Invite him to the table."

Although I was tired, I still had hopes of meeting the man I had seen. I turned to look again for him, but he had disappeared. I guessed it was not to be.

"Jane," Annie was saying. "I'd like you to meet my friend Andy and his friend Ernie. They are in town from New Jersey and just finished dinner."

I looked up and said hello, but I could not see his friend's face. Then he turned around. It was the man from the bar. I almost knocked over the teapot.

"Jane, be careful," Annie said.

"Sorry," I mumbled. "So sorry," as I grabbed a napkin and patted the wet spot next to my plate.

"No problem," he said with a slight accent. "Let me get another chair."

He pulled one from the next table and put it next to my seat. Annie was already conversing with Andy, and I could talk with the man who had triggered my imagination. There was silence. I sipped more tea. I waited.

He ordered tea and asked me if I wanted anything else.

"No, I am fine," I said. How lame did that sound? Couldn't I think of anything clever to say? I tried to smile but he was looking around the room.

I must be boring him already. Think of something, Jane.

"Where are you from?" I murmured.

"Did you say something?"

He turned to me, and his eyes were deep brown and almond shaped—almost Asian with a slight slant.

"Where are you from?" I asked. "You have a slight accent."

He smiled. "I'm from Cuba. Do I still sound like Ricky Ricardo?"

I laughed. He seemed to relax. "No, no," I said.

"Well with your red hair, you could be my Lucy."

By then we were both laughing.

He told me he had been in this country since he was nineteen years old and had escaped from Cuba on a boat with people from the Catholic Church. He had spent his early years in Miami and then moved to New Jersey to live with his cousin and learn English. He said his life in Cuba had been very difficult and coming to the US had always been his dream. The rest of his family stayed behind, but he had hopes they would come to the United States some day.

I tried to practice my Spanish with him, and it just made him laugh. My accent was "very American," he said, and he promised if I spent time with him, he would make it more "Cuban." I smiled. It was easy with him.

He looked at me when we spoke and the eye contact was warm. I sensed a genuine interest when I talked about my art and my work. I told him about an upcoming show at the Javits Center, and he said to be sure to invite him.

A tap on the shoulder— "Jane." Annie pressed my arm. "We have to leave."

I looked up. I had not even realized how quickly the time had gone. It was 1:00 a.m.

Ernie stood up. His friend was walking Annie to the door. I pushed my chair back and grabbed my jacket. He offered to help me put it on. Standing next to him, I felt a tingle inside me. His arms were very long and muscular, and as I slid into my jacket, I brushed against his chest. No flab there—nothing like my mushy stomach. *If I date this man*, I thought, *I better get back into the pool and do my laps.*

"It was a pleasure meeting you." He was saying as Annie and I got into a cab.

"I'll call you," Andy said to Annie.

Nothing more from Ernie but a wave of the hand. I smiled wistfully and waved back.

That was the end of that.

ଔ

By the time Ernie finally called me, I was dealing with both family and business upheavals. It was therefore a welcome surprise to hear that "Ricky Ricardo" voice on the phone. We talked and he casually suggested we go out Friday night for dinner and dancing. I'd always thought of Friday as the "second night" of the weekend, and Saturday the prime "date night," so I assumed he had something else to do Saturday, and I would be second best. I agreed to go anyway.

I wanted to get away from all the problems with my life at that moment, and a date would be a good distraction, so I gave him directions to my apartment. At the time, I was living on the Upper East Side of Manhattan and he had to drive in from New Jersey. Meeting at nine o'clock would give him enough time to finish work and relax before dinner. I thought how great it would be to go out and just unwind.

The first thing I discovered about Ernie that night was that he was always late. I have often been known to be a "little" late, but not *always* late—Ernie was *always* late. Secondly, he was the most fabulous dancer I had ever been out with. Perhaps his Latin heritage gave him his natural grace. I did not know, but he could move on the dance floor. And third, I learned he was in construction and truly did not have an ounce of fat on his body. How could I keep up? More importantly, he liked to read and enjoyed talking about different subjects. He seemed to have some firm opinions, but also did not seem unreceptive to listening and changing. I liked that about him because he made me feel that he would listen to my thoughts and consider them. This openness made for an immediate warmth between us and led to pleasant evenings.

I did not envision that Ernie would be the "man in my life" forever. I enjoyed his company and I loved going dancing with him on Friday nights—I was still *second* and he was still late. But instead of seeing him once every three or four weeks, we were starting to see each other every other week. My business problems were becoming unmanageable, and I knew I could not maintain my Upper East Side rent. I would have to move. I did not share any of this with him. He thought I had talent, and I did not want him to think I was unsuccessful. I still felt insecure and scared about my future. It was a low point in my life and seeing him provided a bright spot in my world.

And then it ended.... He stopped calling.

We had a fabulous evening and I thought we had taken steps forward in our relationship. We were closer physically, and I had shared some of my problems with him. He had advised me to look at my situation objectively and not be afraid to make changes. I remember him holding me and kissing the top of my head while telling me to take a chance on something new. It was nice to open myself a little to someone who seemed receptive. I was looking forward to our time together until it stopped....

೫

Months passed and there was no Ernie. I prepared to move, restarted my business in a new direction, and coped with the disappointment of his absence. I had looked forward to those Friday nights and missed his presence. It angered me that he simply stopped calling, but I had to accept it. I was very busy breaking into the embellished tee shirt business and trying to earn a living. Besides, I told myself it had only been a fun relationship, nothing serious, so let it go. And I did....

Ernie came back into my life with a phone call as if no time had passed.

"Hello, how you doing? It's Ricky Ricardo."

"Huh," I said. He laughed and started talking. It had been six months since our last evening together, and I was not going to make it easy for him. I pretended I did not know who he was, and in time, he sounded a little nervous. I turned down his request to see me that Friday and told him to call me the following week as I had a wholesale trade show coming up and was busy. Do you think he called the next week? No—but he did call the following week and asked me out for Saturday night—that I accepted.

C**ʒ**

The details of my relationship with Ernie could fill a romantic novel, but all I can tell you is that he became the "significant other" in my life. What started out as a strong physical attraction turned into a supportive, caring companionship between two people. Although we were lovers, we did not live together. That was my choice since I worked in my home and it would have been difficult to have someone else there. But his presence in my life helped give me the confidence to attempt the things I did. There were always ups and downs, but having someone believe in me, no matter how many flaws I had, made my life so much easier. I had finally found my best friend and I was *so* grateful.

~ ~ ~

...*Streets filled with torn newspapers, garbage reeking of rotting vegetables, piles of dog feces in the gutter, milk spilled on the curbs.*

...*A gunshot coming from the club at 4:00 in the morning, drunk patrons streaming out of bars yelling and fighting with each other.*

...*Prostitutes walking 46th Street at 5:00 in the morning dressed in high white boots, short black leather miniskirts, and black bras.*

...*The sound of a police siren....*

This was to be my new Manhattan neighborhood.

"HELL'S KITCHEN"

Hell's Kitchen

Can you imagine choosing to live in a neighborhood nicknamed "Hell's Kitchen"? Probably not—but that is where I ended up. When I chose to move to West 43rd Street, I had no idea that the area had been made famous by the "Westies" gang. Apparently, they ruled that part of town for years, and even the midtown police force had trouble dealing with them. But during the day, it looked peaceful enough and the area was being redeveloped, so the new buildings had reasonable rents. They were also beautiful and their proximity to the Lincoln Tunnel, which goes into New Jersey (where Ernie lived), was another plus. The garment center—West 34th to 40th Street—was within walking distance, and the revitalized Broadway theater district was only three blocks away. What a great place to find.

The apartment, although small, had enough room for me to create a working studio. It was on the tenth floor of a luxury high-rise, which had a concierge to receive guests and packages. No more climbing stairs with bags of clothes, displays, and fabrics. The doorman would help us with packages, and we could take an elevator upstairs. The apartment had large panoramic windows and a small balcony. The building also had a rooftop gym with a small pool and even a common room for entertaining. But the most amazing part of all was the nighttime views of Manhattan. From my window, the fading sun hitting the buildings created adobe red, turquoise blue, and liquid gray images of a bouncing skyline. I could relax there and be inspired to create "New York City" art.

When I first moved in, there were still prostitutes and noisy nightclubs in the area, but with time, the revitalization of Times Square extended to 10th and 11th Avenues and the neighborhood transitioned from "Hell's Kitchen" to "Clinton." There are still pockets of undeveloped and darkly lit streets, but now there are luxury high-rises all over. Ninth Avenue is filled with restaurants and tourists looking for the flavor of New York. The building complex across the street from my apartment houses neighborhood Broadway and film actors. Movie crews use our cross streets for location shoots all the time. One day you might see Al Pacino in animated conversation with his friends sitting outside the Little Pie Company enjoying coffee and a delicious pastry. The aroma of freshly baked pies is always on 43rd Street as well as the smell of the healthy food cooked daily at the restaurant, Good 'N' Plenty. Jane Krakowski of *30 Rock* and actress Anne Meara have both smiled at me as they ate their meals there. Down the block, Justin Timberlake opened a Southern restaurant, and the younger, celebrity-oriented crowd packs it every night. Zen Palette on the corner of 46th Street has vegetarian food where I once spotted Ben Vereen on his cell phone. On 42nd Street, West Bank Café is always filled with the before-theater crowd, and after the shows, many Broadway stars go there to unwind. Steve, the owner, has always been a big supporter of my charity work and created a cabaret there named after my dear friend Laurie Beechman. I so enjoy eating there with friends and family.

I have come to know all these places, and the people who work there are now a part of my life. Because Manhattan is so large and populated, there is something warm and comforting about going to the same place every day and being greeted by people you know. It really is easy to get lost in the city. But the warmth of someone saying, "Hi Jane, do you want the same thing?" has helped me adjust to the anonymity of Manhattan. These relationships, although seemingly superficial, have played a very important part in making me feel as if my Manhattan neighborhood is my home.

Moving Forward

The second and third years of the fashion show were years of growth. I met a wonderful actress named Loyita Woods, who would become a most cherished friend and supporter. Her husband, Robert S. Woods, played Bo Buchanan on *One Life To Live*. Mom and I had watched him for years, and I hoped Loyita could entice him to participate in our next group of shows. Luckily, she did.

Rita Salk had found us some wonderful new daytime stars and we were excited. *Oh my God*—there would be a lot of people: Liz Vassey from *All My Children,* who later went out to Hollywood; Tonya Walker from *One Life To Live*; Jean Carol, Michael Palance, from *One Life To Live*, etc.

I was a huge fan of James Horan from *Loving* as I found him both sexy and dangerous and wanted him to be a model, as well, but Rita Salk had been unable to reach him. By chance, I had one of my first "fan encounters." My mother had taken a train in from Florida, and I went to pick her up at Penn Station in New York City. Unfortunately, she had an accident going down the escalator after arriving, and we had to call for assistance to get her to a hospital.

We were approaching St. Vincent's in the ambulance when I recognized a tall, lanky, and handsome man walking by the hospital. The moment the ambulance door opened, I raced out and pursued the man whom I recognized as James Horan, leaving a stunned mother and the EMTs glaring after me. When I caught up to him, I tapped him on the back. He turned and looked at me, and I couldn't speak. Finally, I told him who I was, and that Rita Salk had tried to reach him to participate in my fundraiser. I told him I had left my injured mother when I saw him. We laughed together, and he promised to check his schedule and let me or Rita know if he could attend. I thanked him and ran back to Mom who forgave me for leaving her as she was an even bigger fan than I was. The pain of her injury seemed to lessen as she envisioned him participating in the show...of course, he did participate and made a point of greeting her.

ଓ

I always assumed that stars had a say in how their characters dressed, but I learned that year that wasn't always the case. On television Tonya Walker, who played Alex Olanov on *One Life To Live* often dressed in very alluring outfits. So when we designed the outfits for the stars, we assumed Tonya would want to wear our sexiest items. At that time, we were making lots of nightwear, camisoles, and beautiful cover-ups. We also had a magnificent velvet cocoon embellished with vintage antique flowers that we put over these sexy silk items. When we showed Tonya these pieces, she said, "Oh no. I don't dress like that. I would like to be more conservative."

Okay, so we gave her some beautiful Victorian blouses and long skirts and shirts to wear. This pleased her, and we were set to go.

The day of the fashion show, we had our backstage crew ready, the outfits tagged and labeled with each star's name, and we had rehearsed in our minds the order of the fashions. Tonya, who had eschewed our sexy items for a conservative dress, came that day with a very different agenda. When we gave her our outfits, she said, "Don't worry, I'm prepared." When it came time to model the clothes, she decided to wear some of her own undergarments.

Instead of the cocoon being worn with a tank top or shirt, Tonya came out (with her escort, Bob Woods) in a black bustier and very short skirt. She proceeded to shock both Bob Woods and me by removing the cocoon and tossing it onto the floor. That for me was one of my first lessons in understanding actors. To say that was the highlight of that show would be an understatement.

When I made that initial phone call to the Leukemia Society, I did not have any long-range agenda planned. I did not even think about making this an annual calling. I wanted to contribute something because I was financially unable to write a significant check. But I never expected what happened next.

Even though that year would prove to be our most successful to date, we could no longer return to the Pursuits Disco at the Hilton. The hotel wanted a new restaurant there, and the disco would be closed. I did not know where else we could go. For the first time, we had some publicity in a soap magazine and daytime stars were more anxious to participate. We tried to make things as easy as possible for them in terms of time and commitment. Rita Salk was also helping us, and because of my friendship with Loyita and Bob Woods, we had established a good foothold in the daytime community. But we had no place to hold the event.

Rita Salk had an outreach network all over the public relations community. It seemed like she knew everyone in the daytime world as well as many in other fields of entertainment. One of the people she knew was a gentleman named Clyde Duneier. He was a very influential person in the jewelry business. He sponsored a fundraiser every year for the Juvenile Diabetes Foundation and had started holding it at a new place in Times Square—the New York Marriott Marquis Hotel. Clyde offered to meet with me and the representatives from the Leukemia Society for lunch at the Friars Club.

Apparently that was a "big deal" because women were usually not allowed at the club. I don't remember very much about that lunch except for how pleasant and helpful Clyde was and that the actor Roger Moore (who played James Bond at that time) stopped at our table to talk to us. He was very tall and dressed in a beautiful gray silk suit. Again, I was speechless and just stared foolishly at him thinking, *Isn't he handsome and gentlemanly?* It was more than I had expected and far outweighed, at that time, the fact that Clyde told us to call Tom Reese at the Marriott and that Tom would find us a place in the hotel to hold our event.

When Clyde suggested we go to the Marriott, I felt a little apprehensive. The Times Square Marriott Marquis was large, very modern, and in an area that had been or was being redeveloped. Forty-second Street at one time was a Mecca for prostitutes, drug addicts, panhandlers, and "night crawlers." People went to the theaters there and then went home. With the opening of this beautiful hotel, New York City hoped to rejuvenate the theater district. The Marriott, the epicenter of this plan, would serve as a forerunner in making Times Square the "crossroads of the world," it is today. Still, at that time, I could not be sure if people would want to come to a benefit in that area. Little did I know then that my life would become irrevocably associated with Times Square.

The next day, Rita called to tell me she had arranged an appointment for the following week with Tom Reese. She thought I should go there with the Leukemia Society representative since she did not wish to attend. That did not make me happy as I was very shy and not adept at meeting new people—especially men in powerful positions. I had always chosen to stay away from the corporate world, and suddenly I had to enter it. *I am not ready to walk in those shoes,* I thought. I knew my legs would be shaky and my throat would get hoarse as I spoke. Nervousness overcame me, and I just sat there thinking about what I might say. Then I remembered that Lynn, from the Leukemia Society, would be with me and I relaxed. She could do the talking, negotiating, etc., and I could simply sit there and nod or smile.

I told Rita this, and she laughed and said, "Jane, your new life is just beginning. Get used to it."

Not so fast.

The Meeting

It was an afternoon meeting, and I did not know what to wear. I shocked myself by choosing "Pucci"-style leggings and a black tee shirt top. It was warm out and I wanted to be comfortable. I brought with me two samples of Jane Elissa clothing and some photos of our designs worn by celebrities. I did not bring much because I did not want to appear too anxious. We waited outside Mr. Reese's office for a short time, and then his secretary invited us in. His office was large and filled with Marriott acknowledgments on the wall. He was a tall, gray-haired, pleasant-looking man with a warm smile and a hearty handshake. I later learned his suit—a blue silk pinstripe, tailored to fit, with a yellow tie—represented traditional attire for corporate America. He invited us to sit down, and Lynn began telling him about our event. Apparently, he knew all about it as he had been prepped by both Clyde and Rita. He suggested we tour the hotel and see if he could come up with a room for the event.

We saw all the ballrooms and workrooms that the hotel had to offer. Mr. Reese's suggested we do a Sunday afternoon event in the hotel's Astor Ballroom. He thought a buffet luncheon with a fashion show would work well. The small anteroom would serve as the buffet area, and we could use the larger room with theater-style seating for the show. They would build a T-shaped stage area with a podium for the emcee. The actors and models would come from the "kitchen area" and that would be the changing room. The Green Room would be the bathroom and connected sitting area next to the kitchen entrance so the actors could have lunch and relax before they had to go out and model.

It seemed easy enough from his description, but it made me anxious to have a very small kitchen space for our models. Mr. Reese reassured me, however, that many other companies had done things there, and everything had gone well—it was fine. I thought if everyone thinks it'll work, I'll just have to do my best.

As we were thanking him, he gave us the name and phone number of the banquet manager who would work with us and smiled broadly, shaking our hands. We thanked him again, and I thought the meeting was over, but Mr. Reese asked me to stay as he wanted to give me a further tour of the hotel. I looked at Lynn and nervously agreed. She left after we made plans to speak in the next few days to finalize the event details.

I could not imagine what Mr. Reese wanted to show me, but I went with him to the eighth floor, where the lobby is located. That surprised me because most lobbies are on the first floor. He wanted me to see their retail operations. He said the hotel had a gift shop, and I assumed he wanted me to see the store. His cordial manner made it very easy for me to chat with him. I thought how lucky the people were who worked with him that he seemed so easygoing. His nature helped me to gradually lose my shyness and even laugh with him about some of my "soap" tales.

We proceeded to the eighth floor, and I noticed that they only had one very large gift shop. The rest of the area consisted of empty space and a desk with an information sign and a smiling person who gave people directions. The check-in area and a restaurant were located across from the elevator. It seemed nice enough to me, but there was an awful lot of empty space. Our next destination, the third floor, housed the entrance to the Marquis Theater. Buried in a corner, off to the left, was a hair salon. The remainder of the space consisted of corporate offices. The hair salon did not seem visible, and Mr. Reese explained that he'd thought about moving it to the first floor, which was in the other walkway on the street. This might generate more business. I nodded and he said, "Let me show you the shops downstairs. One of them is really beautiful."

We went to the first floor on the outside arcade, and I must say he was right. There were two stores there—one, a very upscale leather goods store with beautiful merchandise. The décor consisted of antique wooden displays and even a cherry wood grand piano. I remarked that everything in there must be expensive.

"It mostly is," he replied with a smile.

The other store on the first floor consisted of souvenirs and featured every kind of Broadway related item imaginable. I didn't know much about the souvenir business, but the store did not have an inch without merchandise. Amazingly, it did not look crowded, just inviting. I thought the two stores offered different kinds of merchandise and probably generated a lot of business. The middle store did not have a tenant and that was where Mr. Reese wanted to put the hair salon. It seemed like a logical place to me, but the eighth floor would have been good also. Once we were finished with our "tour," I wondered where we were going next. He seemed to be waiting for me to say something, but I didn't know what. I just stood there—

"Well, what do you think?" he asked.

"They are great shops."

Again he asked, "So, what do you think?"

Again, I did not know what to say. He stared at the leather goods place as if transfixed in thought before he whirled to me and said, "Well, I'm going to develop the eighth floor. Do you want a store?"

He stared deeply at me and my head went back as I was in shock. I stammered, "Sure, of course, it would be great." I did not really know what I was saying, but I could not say no.

All my life I'd wanted a shop, but I'd imagined a little artsy beach place by the ocean—simple, easy, quiet. Here I was being offered a space in the newest, most visible hotel in Manhattan. Times Square, Broadway, my name up in lights.

What just happened?

The Fourth Year

The benefit that year would be totally different from the previous ones. For one thing, Rita Salk had gotten more involved. We were now serving food and offering the opportunity to bid on donated items in a *very* small silent auction. I had no idea what that was until Lynn from the Leukemia Society suggested we could increase our revenue by asking the stars to bring signed memorabilia. They provided some signed scripts and clothing worn on the show as personal keepsakes. For the auction, we placed sign-in sheets for bids and arranged for someone to close the auction by collecting the papers later. The good thing about this was that it did not cost us anything. It created a way to bring in money and give the bidder something very special. We also had a much longer program because we had over twenty-five daytime stars involved. That meant we had to have enough fashions for them to "strut their stuff" and enjoy themselves. That also required a lot more time for fitting.

All these terrific celebrities were now marching in and out of my apartment for fittings. Each one of them had a different take on their surroundings. Parker Posey, who at that time appeared on *As the World Turns* and is currently a big Indie film star, came into my living room, plopped herself down on the couch and said, "Okay, what do I wear?"

Simple as that.

Melina Kanakaredes, from *Guiding Light*, was as gracious and beautiful as she is now. She easily wore some of the more elegant creations and ended up buying a jacket. (She went on to star in *CSI-New York* and other hit TV series.) Loyita and Bob Woods came over and loved the window area. We made them a jacket for their son Tanner, and they were thrilled. Julie Benz, who has gone on to film and TV stardom, was very young at the time. She had just graduated high school and wanted to go to New York University. Her parents were very supportive, and I thought how lucky she was to have that encouragement. Julie had been a skater, and she wasn't as thin as most of the other actresses so she fretted about that. But she was naturally pretty and a normal size so our clothes looked great on her. She ended up buying some things, as well.

Most of the guys just took whatever I gave them and looked fabulous. They expected that I knew what would look good on them because of my "fashion sense." And that year everyone seemed happy. That was not always the case as you will see in the future.

You can imagine how starstruck we all were initially. But as time went on, the responsibilities of putting a growing show together held precedence over the aura of stardom. It took a lot of work to coordinate twenty-five people in a small kitchen area and have them change twice. Run in, grab clothes, run out, and line up quickly. There were now volunteer dressers, who helped the stars change, and Avé became the backstage coordinator. I went back and forth from the kitchen to the stage to make sure everyone found their place and went out on time.

We had two hosts at the podium. They included Rita Jenrette, who after the debacle of her infamous marriage, wanted to be an actress, and talk show host Lynn Graham (former radio and TV host Virginia Graham's daughter). Lynn had found me at an industry trade show selling my items and became a client and ultimately a friend. Her glibness and sense of humor coordinated well with Rita's commentary. Both needed to be able to ad-lib because at that early stage in our fashion show, we were not experienced in timing. Lynn was terrific at filling empty space by making jokes to keep the audience amused.

One of the motivations for these soap stars to participate and lend their generosity, besides supporting the charity, was the opportunity to be featured in soap magazines. This dimension of the benefit forced me to deal with paparazzi that specifically followed and photographed celebrities for these magazines. My fashion show turned out to be great press because it was celebrities off-the-cuff, wearing colorful items, and donating their time for charity. Everyone gave for the cause. The press was a beneficial by-product for all of us.

As time went on, I learned which celebrities wanted their pictures taken and which ones were not as interested. That helped me manage the press.

One of Rita Salk's celebrity friends was Maria Burton—Elizabeth and Richard Burton's daughter. She lived across the street from my apartment building and at that time worked with her husband Steve Carson managing child talent. She had a daughter Eliza. Maria and I became friends. I never thought of her as Elizabeth's daughter, rather I saw her as a fellow female who had a glamorous mother.

Although my mother was not a movie star, she was the ultimate "glamorous mom." At a young age she had modeled, dabbled in show business, and hosted at a canteen during the war. She was very beautiful and enjoyed the stage. Maria and I spent many hours talking about how having that kind of mother affected being a daughter. Of course, my mother didn't have Elizabeth's status, but growing up with a mother whose image was larger than life was something we shared. I always felt very close to Maria. She has a special place in my heart.

Because Maria had agreed to participate in the fashion show, there was a lot of "buzz" about the event that year. Rita put out press releases and the magazine photographers came. They wanted special seating, interviews, and pictures in the Green Room with the stars. Rita explained to me that this was good because the more press coverage, the more tickets we could sell.

She even wanted them to take pictures of me with the celebrities and interview me. I did not relish that, but it proved to be the beginning of my "press persona," and I had to learn to speak, how to pose, and what to say. I can't tell you I was successful, but I took the first step.

This event was the best one we had. My parents came and were introduced. My father took a bow and my mom got to speak and thank everyone.

The fans were able to see their favorite stars up close and personal and enjoy something that hadn't been done yet with daytime stars. It was really a positive experience for everyone. We started a mailing list, and Lynn from the Leukemia Society asked me if I would do another show the following year. Despite being totally exhausted, I was thrilled at the interest and the success of the event. The Marriott generously underwrote the costs, so all the money raised went to the charity. The year before we had raised five thousand dollars, but that year we gave the Leukemia Society twenty-five thousand.

What a great step up. I felt very proud, and I thanked everyone involved. What I didn't know then, an annual "Jane Elissa Extravaganza" would be around the corner.

Once the fashion show was over, I felt exhausted but also a little bit sad. I had spent almost eight months preparing for the show and now there was an emptiness—as if the space left by the lack of activity would never be filled. I had nothing immediate to throw myself into, and I found that even though I was thrilled with the results of the endeavor, I was disappointed that the phone had stopped ringing. Celebrity fittings were over, photographers wanting pictures, questions and descriptions—all gone. I was a nobody again. It seemed strange and lonely.

On Hold

I had returned to designing my wholesale clothing line when Mr. Reese's office called. They were building another store on the eighth floor, and his attention would be focused on that shop. I would have to wait at least six to twelve months before even planning the opening venue. In the interim, I still had to earn a living, and I couldn't be sure if the store would ever come through. But once the idea of the shop was in my head, it was difficult not to think about what it would be like to own a space in that location. I started having dreams about merchandise and what we could sell there. I also imagined what it might look like and how I would make it profitable. As renowned as we were in the very small art to wear market, we were nobodies in the retail market. How would I do it? Where would the money come from? Who could supply the merchandise? But most of all, would it really happen?

I went back and forth to the Marriott to look at the eighth floor. Within six months, the other store had opened. It sold new antiques—actually reproductions of all old antique furniture, jewelry, lamps, etc. It was a beautiful, large store and it filled a lot of the empty space on that side of the floor. Where did Mr. Reese think he could put me? There was a newly created business center area on the corner opposite the antique store. Next to the center was a Broadway ticket broker. Then came an American Express desk and the Marriott's huge retail store, which sold all kinds of New York City souvenirs. It appeared that there would be no place for me. Some of my so-called friends were telling me it wasn't going to happen. No one gives an "unknown" a prime retail space in the middle of Times Square. Why would Mr. Reese want me in his hotel? Granted, I was manufacturing beautiful one-of-a-kind, handmade items, but so were other people. They were not quite at my level, but I had never tested the retail waters before. And we were in a financial recession in the early 90s. I started to have my doubts.

In the meantime, the Leukemia Society wanted me to continue doing benefits on an annual basis. Kerri Dubler, a new campaign worker, was very enthusiastic about the potential of our event. Although I appreciated their interest, my own future preoccupied my mind, and I did not really want to devote all the time needed to push the event. Nevertheless, Kerri and I sat down one day and mapped out a new plan. We would have an evening show in a ballroom at the Marriott. The Leukemia Society would help get people to come, and I would tap into my new soap friends to form a committee. Kerri suggested we recognize someone from the daytime community for their support of the event. That way we could also get their fans and friends to come. We came up with the Charlotte Meyers Volunteer Recognition award in honor of Mom and her battle with Leukemia, and we chose Loyita and Bob Woods to receive it. They had been so supportive with the development of the fundraiser, and I believed they had earned the honor of being the first recipients.

Loyita was so generous that she offered to help me plan the show. She wanted to make sure it would be the best it could because she believed in the cause, too. I welcomed the help. Loyita, being the consummate organizer, recruited people to help, to model, and to work behind the scenes. She was wonderful.

This was the first time there was a cocktail party before the show and guests had the opportunity to mingle with celebrities. It seemed to be a positive addition to the event as people enjoyed meeting the stars.

Robert S. and Loyita Woods with Charlotte Meyers

Walt Willey "Jackson Montgomery" came and presented Bob and Loyita with the Charlotte Meyers Volunteer Recognition Award, and Mom spoke and thanked everyone. The stars looked fabulous in their outfits, and at the end of the evening, many people approached me and said they would attend the following year. I was so relieved and I thanked Loyita over and over again. Without her, it would have been difficult to put the show together because I was preoccupied with getting the store. I felt as if the Marriott had dangled a carrot in front of me, and I could not stop thinking about it.

When would it happen?

The Shop

"*H*ello Jane, this is Mady from Mr. Reese's office. He would like to see you tomorrow, and he's ready to start construction on your shop. We hope you've been busy making merchandise. Please call us back to confirm a 2:00 p.m. appointment. Thank you"

It was for real. It was going to happen. There would be a Jane Elissa shop in the Marriott Hotel in Times Square in New York City!

No way—

Yes!

Mr. Reese smiled when I came in wearing a red wool Josephine Originals business suit that was designed by one of my close associates. I was shaking and I spoke very little while I followed him to the eighth floor where the business center had been located. The space was waiting for me. We talked about the format, what he wanted the outside to look like in order to conform with the rest of the hotel. Everything else was up to me.

I met the contractor, we mapped it out, and in one month the space was ready. Two-hundred and fifty square feet, with a side room for a sewing machine and a worker, a few storage closets, and a desk for Avé who would run the store as well as create goods in the back. It was ideal. The lease would be for five years with an option to renew. I had to pay for the construction of the store over a two-year time period and provide a two-month security, but the

Marriott offered four months of free rent to get the fixtures, display pieces, and inventory together. I also needed people to help run the store as Mr. Reese wanted it open *every day* from approximately 9:30 a.m. or 10:00 a.m. until at least 8:00 p.m. or 9:00 p.m. That meant double shifts and weekends. There also were matinee days on Wednesday, Saturday, and Sunday which required extra help because groups arrived on busses, and they came to the eighth floor to eat, go to the bathroom, or just enjoy the lobby before their show. It seemed overwhelming.

Everything finally fell in place with a lot of work and help from my dear friend Annie Santiago. Along with my life savings, she provided the seed money to purchase inventory. I paid for everything up front in full without having any debt. I wanted it that way because I was not comfortable carrying debt. All invoices got paid on receipt of goods, which was not a great way to do business I later found out. It would have been better to carry credit so I could sell the merchandise and then pay the bills. That way we could have maintained a solid cash flow, but I didn't know anything about that yet, and I wanted to pay my friend's loan and myself back as quickly as possible.

Friends of mine had suggestions about what to carry, and one of my clients, Helaine Schlar, was a jewelry buyer. She offered to fill a case of jewelry with her special merchandise on consignment. We would do a 50/50 split. Since I knew nothing about buying jewelry, I thought, *okay, we'll give it a try.* She brought very unusual pieces, priced them, and came once a week to refill the case. Within one month, I had her display and another case of jewelry that I found by walking Manhattan and also at wholesale trade shows.

No matter how beautiful everything was in the store, the first thing the women did when they entered was turn to the left to look at the jewelry. It always sold. To this day, I thank Helaine for persuading me to carry jewelry. Now, wherever we do shows, I always have some. If they buy a shawl, I have a beautiful pin for the lapel. For a blouse, they might buy earrings or a bracelet. It's a good business tactic to complete the entire outfit, especially with

handmade pieces that no one else will have.
Lesson learned.

Diane Michaels

I met Diane Michaels soon after I began my fashion events. Tommy Michaels, her son, played Timmy on *All My Children*, and they both were very anxious to help me raise money for leukemia research. Diane was very pretty with strong brown eyes and dark brown hair. She amazed me because she somehow managed to have a job, take her kids to school, and be on set with Tommy when she needed to be there. She juggled everything to help her son launch a career. One thing I noticed about Diane was that she would never push Tommy into doing things. She said if he wanted to continue acting, she would support him, but if not, it was fine with her. She wanted him to complete his schoolwork and to compete in sports when he wanted to. I respected the way she handled her life, and she helped me immensely in launching my benefits.

Diane and Tommy were the first people to take me to the set of *All My Children*. I would go there to accompany her or stay for a while with Tommy if she needed to run an errand. I also networked with celebrities to invite them to participate in the benefits. I met Chris Lawford, Genie Francis, who was on *All My Children* at that time, Lee Meriweather, and even Susan Lucci.

It was quite a treat for me to be in Tommy's dressing room and watch him as he learned his lines for the day. I actually read lines with him—something I'd never thought I would do. Of course, my reading of the other characters was not quite up to an actor's standard, but it did help him to remember the words and also to perfect the nuances of his pronunciation. Although the room was small with a mirror with lights all around it, I felt very tall in there. It was exciting.

I spent a lot of personal time with Diane and Tommy. We even helped move a newly hired John Callahan (Edmund on *All My Children*) into his New York apartment. They were instrumental in getting Meaghan Schick, our leukemia survivor, to participate on stage in the benefits. I saw the inner workings of daytime, not as a fan, but as part of a family, and the stars were very kind to me—especially Ruth Warrick (Phoebe) who would later come to all my benefits and even purchase some of my shawls. She regaled me with the most wonderful stories whenever we met. The door that Diane opened led me into the world of *All My Children,* and I will always be grateful for those precious years we shared. I have lost touch with her since her son left the show but wish them all the best.

Irene Krause, Gabby Winkel, and Pat Sellers

Irene Krause was a featured writer at *Soap Opera Weekly* magazine. She had blue eyes and short brown hair. Her posture and build always struck me; she was very thin and stood so straight that I was a little in awe of her. She had modeled before and approached me about participating in our benefits. Irene was a great asset because she had access to the soap stars, wrote for a magazine, and knew how to model and pose professionally. More importantly, she wanted to help, and we enjoyed talking to each other.

I bonded with Irene as we were both single and dating. She was more anxious to commit to a relationship than I was, but we loved to dish about looking for, finding, and losing love. We spent hours between fashion shows wondering about why men act the way they do. But she always found great guys for our benefits, and she helped all the stars with their "struts" down the runway.

Irene introduced me to Pat Sellers, who wrote for *Soap Opera Weekly* at the time, and who would later become our fashion commentator, client, and most importantly, my friend. *Soap Opera Weekly* always featured photos taken at the event, and Pat usually wrote a tongue-in-cheek column called "Pat's Personal." Gabby Winkel, also introduced to me by Irene, is now at *Soap Opera Weekly* and has been an avid supporter of the Jane Elissa Extravaganza from the beginning.

Many of the missteps of the evening were caught and landed smack in the magazine. But without the support of these reporters, my event would never have grown to the stature it did. Soap fans heard about the fundraisers through the magazines because the press and I worked so closely together.

Photographers, although absolutely necessary to grow an event, can sometimes be difficult. They all need to get their photos into the magazine as quickly as possible, and sometimes they are competing for the same shot. In the beginning, I let everyone come and do whatever they wanted. But when they stepped in front of fans to get pictures by the runway, I had to learn to tell them *no*. It was a difficult process for me because I did not like telling someone they couldn't do something when I needed them to publicize the event, but I had to learn to set boundaries. In some ways I became a tyrant, only allowing them specific times and places to photograph the celebrities. They could no longer interrupt my line-up backstage, pull someone out of their place to take a shot, and delay the show. Nor could they step in front of paying guests by the runway. They had to work within the rules, or they could not attend. Initially my stress level elevated when I saw them. There was some screaming, but ultimately we worked out a comfortable arrangement.

I always allowed the press access to the stars who enjoyed being photographed. One actress posed in a green dress, large shawl, and black beret, and was featured in every magazine—*Star, Enquirer, Soap Weekly, Soap Digest*, etc. That was a great coup for me and for her, and we were thrilled. Casper Van Dien agreed to pose with his shirt open, and he also became a featured actor in many magazines. This free press coverage helped my events grow.

Eventually, Irene did find a man and got married, and Jane Elissa Designs created her wedding dress. She looked beautiful and extremely happy. Pat is also now married and retired from *Soap Opera Weekly*, but Gabby went on to become the executive editor. I was grateful for their continued coverage and interest in my events.

Walt Willey

The growth of my retail business coincided with my greater responsibility to the Leukemia Society. With each fashion show, everyone expected more of me, but I also acquired knowledge each year, which helped in the planning of the events. I always had a representative from the LLS work with me, and I created an event committee. Each fundraiser had a different chairperson. The committee members were also responsible to sell tickets.

Companies known to people on the committee donated raffle and silent auction prizes. We chose honorees from the daytime community for their commitment to charitable causes and an official honorary celebrity chair was brought on. People were becoming excited to get involved with us.

All the performers gave of their time and effort for me and the cause I believed in. I did not realize how amazing that was until I learned how difficult it was to book talent. I was able to deal directly with the artist. It was truly an act of love on everyone's part, and as I look back on it, I do have a sense of pride in all that we accomplished. Perhaps, it was the opportunity to perform that made some come. For others, to be photographed for the magazines was good press, but it did not matter what the motive, everyone was truly there in good spirit.

The actual early year events at the Marriott are grouped together in my mind. Only by looking at the programs, do I remember what years people came. (Yes, we had programs and printed invitations—all donated.) When we honored Loyita and Bob, they introduced me to Walt Willey, Jackson Montgomery on *All My Children.* He told me he would love to help out whenever needed, and I accepted his offer. He was also an artist who had just released a comic book, and I thought the event would be a good way to promote his book.

I spoke to Kerri Dubler about Walt, and she suggested that we take him to dinner to discuss his participation.

The next day, Kerri called him and arranged a dinner date at a restaurant near the *All My Children* studio. Excitement filled me as I was still in my starstruck stage. To me, Walt Willey was a larger than life daytime star. He played opposite Susan Lucci's Erica Kane, and no one was or *is* bigger than Erica, except a tall, 6'4" and gorgeous Walt Willey with a wonderful sense of humor.

Walt arrived a little late because of his shooting schedule, but I didn't mind because it gave me more time to prepare. When he walked in, he immediately made us feel at ease by joking that we were the only people in the restaurant, and that was how it stayed through dinner. He told us about the day on the set, and he filled us in on his checkered background. He also told us that he enjoyed doing charity work because it gave him an opportunity to let people know that even if they didn't start out on a straight and narrow path, they could still turn their life around and achieve success as he had.

Kerri then told him that we were planning to have another fundraiser and that we would like to honor him. He started laughing and asked us what for? I told him that he had really helped us the year before, and I knew about his Willey World charities, and I thought he deserved to be recognized. He stared at me intently. Then he pulled something from his pocket, took out a pen, and said, "Who do I make a check out to?"

I said, "No, No. You don't have to donate anything. Giving of your time and lending your name is enough."

He shook his head. "No. Here is a check to the Leukemia Society. Now, you can honor me. At least I've done something."

Still protesting, Kerri took the check. I had no idea how much it was for, but up until that point no other celebrity had given us anything (other than Loyita and Bob Woods, but they were friends) and I was shocked. I remember thinking that he was a special person and how lucky we were to have him as an honoree.

We started talking about the event, and he told us about a group of soap stars who could sing and that they traveled to different venues to perform. He promised to ask them if they would like to entertain at the event, and if they did, he would put together that part of the show. I was thrilled! That would allow me to concentrate on the fashions and other things we would be doing. All in all it was a terrific dinner. He even drove me home with a good-bye kiss on the cheek. That night I was in heaven. The hell part of it started later on.

⌈⌉

Walt had given us a check for five thousand dollars. That was wonderful. We then had money to help defray the cost of the event. Kerri suggested we try and get a sponsor in the future so it could be "underwritten," which meant that we would have someone to cover the out-of-pocket costs. Kerri also taught me to get *everything* donated—from the invitations, to the flowers, to any prize, goodie bags, etc. We had never thought about this before, but we were growing and to add more revenue to the event, we had to have other enticements. We also needed to reach a wider audience. Up until then, most of the people coming had been my clients, friends, and some soap fans. Rita explained that reaching more fans through word of mouth would elevate the event. We needed to get promos in magazines, newspapers, radio, and even on television. And she wanted me to do this with a soap star. Again, I reminded her of my shyness. I did not want to do this, but if it was necessary, I told her I would do it.

⌈⌉

The same year as Walt's event a health crisis came into my life. I had to have surgery and would be unable to get out of bed and around for at least a month. I was homebound and had to work on the fundraiser from my apartment. Walt putting the musical part of the show together was a big help. I still worked with my chairman on the committee, but now most everything was done by phone calls. Avé remained in the store and met with some of the soap stars for their fittings. When I felt better, I actually helped out, but I was in a lot of pain and often uncomfortable. I pushed myself, but at the end of the day, I was exhausted and I could not give my business enough attention. Luckily, we found other manufacturers of merchandise for the store so we did not have to rely so heavily on Jane Elissa one-of-a-kind items. The jewelry and handmade souvenirs got us through.

The evening fundraisers were now in two rooms: buffet dinner and meet-and-greet in one room, and stage and theater-style seating in the other. The Marriott offered us an afternoon of tasting to choose the menu. I always brought along committee members to make the selections. As I have many food allergies and have always battled IBS, I thought this was the best way to select food for other people. My committee loved it because many of them enjoyed seeing how the plates were decorated, what color tablecloths and napkins to choose, and what floral arrangements would work on the tables. Selecting these things was a new chore added to the growing responsibilities I had. Recovery was exhausting, so that year, every task, enjoyable or not, felt like a burden.

CB

We had an abundance of models, wonderful soap singers and no hostess. Robin Strasser from *One Life to Live* volunteered, but she had a difficult task. Everything in the fashion portion was evolving. At the show, I sat down with her and wrote a lineup.

I had assumed that soap actors knew all the other actors on different programs—a little naive of me, wouldn't you know?

Robin wanted to be sure everyone's name was correct. I could not promise her that things wouldn't change at the last minute, so she came up with a brilliant plan. As each actor came out, they would take the microphone and introduce themselves—that way there would be no mistakes. I have to say, that was a stroke of genius because, as part of our auction the prior year, we had given a guest the opportunity to participate in the fashion show, and the lovely winner's name would have totally stumped Robin. There were also some Broadway stars included whom Robin might not have known. A disaster was averted.

Still, other problems popped up that night.... Walt's performers came out first. That left twenty-five soap actors all dressed and waiting in a line (sort of) backstage. They needed to not speak because the audience sat right next to the curtains. Unfortunately, they were ready way too soon. Walt's singers were fine, but long...and longer...and longest. The show's timing needed work, and the actors were anxious to get their job done and be finished. Barbara Beroff, who helped us backstage, constantly asked everyone to be quiet, but it became impossible. I kept running back and forth to the curtain to tell them to cut a little and they tried, but it was still long. I blame myself because I should have gone over everything with Walt in advance.

Although the actors backstage did their job beautifully when it came to modeling, they could not wait to leave. Some of them had early calls the next day, and I let them slip out before the finale. Others like Windsor Harmon (who was new to the business) seemed to have a good time. On the runway, he accompanied the guest bidder and then took off his tee shirt and threw it to a fan for a five hundred dollar donation. Scott Bryce and Brooke Alexander made the perfect couple down the runway, and fans applauded wildly.

Nathan Fillion came out carrying one of the soap vixens, and Robert Cuccioli and Catherine Hickland were a matched cowboy and cowgirl. Shawn Christian and Amy Carlson were playful and even enticed one lady to join them on stage. For the audience that stayed, the show was fabulous. For us behind the scenes, there were torn pages of lineups, clothes on the floor, and worn out voices as well as feet. I had to have a better plan the following year. I would have to learn how to time an event. That would come to me the year we honored Laurie Beechman.

LEA YANG & NATHAN FILLION

The Fear of Success

There were so many things I had to master along the way to build the Extravaganza into a yearly event. Besides the obvious, like sponsors, prizes, and participants, there were the hidden things for which I was unprepared such as an audience that was too noisy or models who had to leave early. When you have twenty or thirty people every year who are working with you on a volunteer basis, you have to know how to be calm even when you are nervous, angry, or just plain tired.

Not being a real people person, I had to break a protective shell I had cultivated all my life. I preferred being the background person, not first in line; however, it was my name on the event, and I was the head of the soiree. I do not know what made me grow into a person who could call people for donations, meet with celebrities and get along with them, sign my name to a contract and be responsible for the money, even if we *did not* sell out the event (That happened once.), and handle angry people if I could not pay them immediately. If a celebrity promised an auction package and it did not happen, I had to try and calm the winner. Usually this did not happen, but at times it did, and I had to enlist another celebrity to fulfill the obligation. Along with being the Jane Elissa of the eighth floor shop, it was so much to take on, that I went into therapy to try and deal with the stress.

One of my clients recommended a therapist her husband

knew who dealt with some of the issues I was facing. He had an office downtown, and he could see me in the middle of the day. The only glitch for me with him was the elevator that went to his office. The office was on the fifth floor and the stairway was usually locked. I have a fear of elevators, which started when, as a child, I was stuck in one, and this elevator held only two people at a time. I had to fight the urge to escape every time I went in by myself. Some days, I got to my appointment early because I wanted to make sure someone else was in the elevator with me. I have since worked on this phobia. I cannot say it has been conquered, but I am better.

The bigger issue, however, was how to manage a growing fund-raising commitment and a business that needed my attention. I enjoyed the excitement of fundraising, but the store and the wholesale business paid the bills. Could the two of them co-exist? How would I become the kind of person who was not ill at ease in a room with hundreds of people and could smile without wanting to run and hide? Small talk would never be my forte, but a least being comfortable in the room and being in charge was something I wanted to learn.

Dr. Wiener turned out to be the perfect person for me. I went to therapy for four years, on and off. I learned a lot about myself. Anyone who thinks the therapist gives you answers is greatly mistaken. The answers come from inside. And more often than not, they are answers you never knew you would give. I was prepared to take that walk into my subconscious because a part of me was very happy having a shop and working on the shows. I could use my grade school and high school theatrical training, and even my singing, when planning the shows. My clothes were on all the models. More people were now interested in shopping in our store and buying my creations. It was a win-win opportunity. What was holding me back?

They say there is something called *fear of success*. For me, it was very real and still is. I learned in therapy that I had to see myself as a person who deserved success. I had worked hard, given of my time, energy, and talent to help others, and created magical clothing. There were people who seemed to like me, and I was sharing my hobbies with others. I even had Ernie in my life, and he cared for me and wanted to help me become better at everything I was doing. It was too much good...when would the roof fall down, or customers stop coming into the shop, or people cease to like me? What would it be like to fail? I had done that before in business, and somehow I had picked myself up and restarted—to be bigger and more visible. What was the fear based on?

After a series of sessions, I discovered that I had been taught to "hide" in my family, and that although on the surface it seemed like my parents supported me (I had all those wonderful lessons.), there was an underlying tension with my mother. I do not blame her for having a need for the spotlight. I unconsciously cleared the way all the time for her to have it. I had learned young not to compete. It was my choice to think I was protecting my mother from having a daughter who would eventually eclipse her spotlight. After all, it was she who had leukemia and the award was named after her. I was still following the path to make *her* recognized. I was reluctant to take it on my own. It was only when Dr. Wiener explained to me about the words *success identity* that I began to see my true path.

At first, I would repeat those words to myself over and over again. What did it mean? Who was I becoming? What connoted success? How would I be successful? Was I already successful? How do you wear success? First, you must take it on from the outside, put it on like clothes, and act the part. That is what I did. I acted like a successful person. What does that mean, you ask? For me it meant I had to envision my life in all the positive states. I took on a cloak of "outer" success. I could no longer walk around with my torn camouflage jacket that I wore when I went hunting for bargains at a flea market. I had to have a new coat. I needed to give myself a fresh and professional outward appearance so that when people met me, I represented the image of what the owner of a fashionable store should look like. That coat—a full length purple-sheared designer mink that I found at a furrier who I did some work for—was a sample—one-of-a-kind—and it became a symbol to me of a first step to seeing myself differently. Today, many people do not wear mink for animal protection reasons, but at that time, it was something many women coveted.

I don't want people to think, *Oh, how shallow. She went out and bought a mink and now she thinks she's a success.* That was not the case. The fur was like *Joseph and the Amazing Technicolor Dream Coat*—it transformed me. When I looked at it, I saw a different person. This outward symbol became the means to finding a healthy, positive image of myself. I would look at my name outside the store, and I would look around me and think—where was this Jane Elissa? Oh—she's right here—she is *me*.

It was okay to say this is *me*. It did not make me "stuck up" or "better" than anyone; it just made me Jane Elissa, the artist who had achieved a goal—she had her own store. It was a good thing.

I spent many years working on the idea of success identity, and even today when I am down, I hold onto the fact that I have achieved something in life. It didn't have to be a great big thing; it could be a small step, but the important thing was to allow myself to enjoy my achievement and to *own* it. You are truly what you become—but you have to let yourself *become* that person. Over the years, I have watched many of the celebrities who participated in our fashion shows become big stars—Julie Benz in Hollywood, Melina Kanakaredes on TV, Josh Duhamel in movies, Amy Carlson in *Blue Bloods,* Kelly Ripa on *Regis and Kelly....* These people have taken their energies and talents and made their dreams happen. I have learned to believe in myself enough to *want* to be more and do more in life. That's what we all need to feel. To be satisfied, to be grateful for what we are given, and to use whatever gifts we have to make life better for ourselves and for others. That desire to do more kept me going from event to event.

The hiccups would come later.

Jean Rooney

*A*fter the previous year's event, I received a phone call from a woman named Jean Rooney. She worked at a securities company and had attended one of our fashion shows. Ilene Butler's husband's company worked with her boss, and he had purchased a table for the women in the office. Jean was a huge fan of Walt Willey and wanted to get involved with the fundraiser. She offered to come to some committee meetings and see how she could help us. I asked her to meet with me at the shop and we'd have dinner together. She agreed.

Jean was a tall thin, blue-eyed, redhead with a warm smile. She came in wearing a fitted cream-colored suit with a cream shirt. She had a matching cream purse and shoes, and she carried a dark brown leather briefcase. She was totally "put together" as they say in the fashion industry, and she went directly to our jewelry case when she entered the store. By now we had so much unusual jewelry that there really was something for everyone. Avé and Jenelle, our intern, were behind the counter, and Jean chose a seed pearl necklace she said she needed for a gift. I told her we would give her a discount, but she insisted on paying the price as marked. She said the price already seemed discounted, which was true.

The items in my store, if purchased in other stores would have cost much more because I was very conservative in my mark-ups.

People often said, "Things are going to be more expensive because it's in a hotel" when they walked in the store, and I wanted people to know our prices were very fair. I also made a lot of the merchandise, so I had some leeway in setting the retail price. Jean's sense that our jewelry was discounted made me think she was a savvy shopper and a smart woman.

Her addition to the committee brought needed changes to the event. She worked directly with the boss of a small Wall Street securities company and asked him to sponsor the event. This gave us an opportunity to reach a new group of people who had never heard of us or what we were trying to do. Jean was able to obtain new prizes, find another printer, call people she knew for flowers and favors and eventually goodie bags. She also knew people who could "buy tables" and that meant we could have assigned seating and perhaps have the show in the same room as the buffet. When you sell tables, you can make more money by commanding a higher price for the seats closer to the stage. And we also now had a program where people could salute the honorees and buy advertising for their company. With Jean in charge of these responsibilities, I was able to concentrate more on the show and the themes I was working on for my fashion segments. I wanted to bring in different styles of clothing for the people who were coming every year.

Catherine Hickland was a fellow Aquarian and a real people person. She had taken me to see *Joseph and the Amazing Technicolor Dream Coat* with Michael Damian, who came to my shop to do a photo shoot to promote my event. She also enjoyed my clothes, and we spent many lunches discussing life, philosophy, and just plain girl talk. She had begun starring in *Les Miserables*, and I wanted to recognize her charitable contributions, so she and Thom Christopher from *One Life To Live* were our next award winners. Since Catherine was in *Les Miserables*, she wanted to bring the people from her show along to do a Broadway singing segment. Nothing could have pleased me more. Although I love Walt dearly, I thought he would be a better host than coordinator of the music and he agreed. He has become the emcee of the Jane Elissa Event over the years and a person who I respect and adore. His commitment to charities and to my efforts has been unwavering and voluntary. His sense of humor has served us well over the years as the "by the seat of our pants" aspect of the fashion show has never fully changed.

Since Catherine had organized the Broadway section, I decided to format the show in two parts. The first was the fashion segment moderated by Pat Sellers. The intermission would be a live auction. The second part would be Broadway performances from Catherine's group, and I had to work with her on the sound system and the lighting, and the audio visuals were very important. The Marriott people were adept at this job. We needed a piano on stage and there was an expense to move and tune it. "No need to panic," I told myself. We have a sponsor and some of the new expenses will be covered.

Jean's first introduction to Walt Willey left her speechless and me laughing. I remembered what a fan I was as well, but now I had become less "in awe" of the actors and more practical about my job. But Jean was so excited to be a part of the event, that she brought new positive energy to that night. Her people greeted her and thanked her for inviting them. They seemed anxious to bid on the auction items, and their presence helped us earn more money than the previous year.

Walt was his usual hysterical self as the emcee, and he got people to bid on packages when they seemed to be ready to take a bathroom break. He caught one woman as she was walking out and made her come back to her seat to bid. It was funny to watch. No one was immune if they put up their hand to bid. Even my brother's friend Bruce, who had come with Joel, got roped into bidding. The next thing he knew he had won a Liberty Helicopter ride around Manhattan.

I named the fashion show "Remembrances of Romance," which was the original theme of our shop, and it fit well with the Broadway segment Catherine did. Louise Sorel (Vivian from *Days of Our Lives*) was a luminous addition to our lineup along with Sal Vaccarino from *One Life To Live,* who had a blast wearing our sequined vests and hat, and Bill Christian from *All My Children*. Yvonne Perry ran late so Kelli Taylor from *All My Children* covered her fashion segment. Kelli wore a long green dress, embroidered beret, and magnificent vintage black embroidered shawl. In that outfit, she was photographed and appeared in every magazine that received it. Her substitution turned out to be a bonus of publicity for her, and she thanked me over-and-over again.

Tonya Walker presented Thom Christopher the Charlotte Meyers Volunteer Recognition Award. His acceptance speech was very gracious. I gave Catherine her award. That first time on stage alone was a big step for me, but I wanted to do it. We had become friends, and I wanted her to know how much I appreciated her efforts. Although I was uncomfortable at first, I relaxed as I read my speech. Catherine made it easy because she just came over and hugged me, and I forgot all about the audience as it became a personal moment between the two of us.

The Broadway performers, including Ron Bohmer, Craig Schulman, and Craig Rubano from *Les Miz* were beyond phenomenal. I snuck out from backstage to hear them, and their voices were so clear I was proud to be standing there. The audience was witnessing a private Broadway moment, and I hoped they understood how lucky they were to be seeing such talent. Catherine had done a wonderful job in selecting the songs and our volunteer pianist, Neil Berg, had worked really well with the actors. I could not have been happier.

After the event, people who I had never met before, were coming up to me and thanking me for inviting them. The aura in the room seemed positive, and there were lots of hugs for everyone. The Broadway stars stayed to meet with the guests and even some of the daytime actors posed for photos. Catherine's husband, Michael E. Knight, who plays Tad on *All My Children*, had to leave quickly because he had to be on set the next morning by 7:30 a.m., but Catherine stayed and mingled. Jean was very happy and told me she would love to start working right away on the next year's show.

I just needed to go home and sleep....

Clint Holmes

*I*n the early 1990s, I had seen an evening talk show with a host named Clint Holmes. Not only was he able to communicate well with his guests, but he also had a wonderful singing voice. He could entertain and I thought he would be a perfect host for my events. I asked Rita Salk to try and find him to see if he would be willing to host the fashion show.

She said, "Jane," in her southern accent. "The man has a top-rated local television show. How am I going to get him to host this? I don't think we're ready."

My answer: "Then he'll just have to make us ready."

That's exactly what he did.

℀

The phone rang.

"Jane, it's Rita. I don't know, dahling, but the gods must be smiling on you. I found Clint's publicist who put me through to Clint. After he asked, 'Who are you?' I worked my charm. He's going to do it. He'll meet you in your shop next week, and dahling, you better be prepared."

A long sign of relief—we would be taking a step up.

℀

Clint Holmes *loved* my shop. He arrived with his wife, and he had a great appreciation for the eclectic mix of merchandise. It was as if he thought my talent equaled his.

With time, I had found menswear designers who made unusual shirts. Joyce and Jacquee were manufacturers and importers of menswear from Paris. Some of the shirts were runway items—strictly one-of-a-kind, and others were part of a line they produced and sold to stores. One of the shirts they created was the "puffy shirt" that Jerry Seinfeld wore on his sitcom. Jacquee was always pleasant to us and sold us samples at a discounted price. We would walk down 8th Avenue into his showroom and come out with bags of merchandise for the shop. I even took Keith Hamilton Cobb (Noah on *All My Children*) up there for a photo shoot for *Soap Opera Weekly*, and he chose some shirts for his own wardrobe. These were the items that the male actors modeled, and Clint loved one shirt that had a guitar on it. My friend Howard, from Stellair Designs, did beautiful airbrushing for us on many of the men's shirts and jackets. He also did some work on the women's items as well.

We had the products to make the show a success, but the most important thing, however, was to make sure Clint would be comfortable in front of our audience as well as enjoy himself on stage. One thing I had to have for him was a much tighter show. I knew I would be putting a lot of pressure on myself.

I was *not* a trained producer, but I had to sit down with Clint and *plan* the show. Somebody had to get a message across. This was a fundraiser, and for all the fun we had meeting and seeing celebrities, we also had to be aware of the main reason we were there—which was to wipe out leukemia. I learned from Clint that pacing was key to putting together a show. We needed an ebb and a flow, and we wanted to keep people watching and listening. If people talked too much, the audience would tune out. If there were too many models in a parade, people would lose interest. The good thing was that the press coverage had created a "buzz" about the benefit and new fans were attending. The stars were doing something different and fans could actually *meet* their favorites.

I had also been introduced to a young leukemia survivor by my brother Joel. His friend's niece Meaghan Schick, as a young child, had an acute form of leukemia, and Joel felt the family would love to get involved with the fundraiser. I thought this would be a good thing because people could learn from Meaghan's experience and see the benefit of our work and their generosity. She became my "poster child," and as I watched her grow at all my events, I marveled at her courage in facing her disease. I also saw her beguile Walt and other celebrities as she became enamored of the theater and performing. She began taking singing lessons and even sang comfortably on our stage. It was a long way from our hospital visit to see her doctor for checkups where they had harvested her healthy bone marrow in case she became ill later in life. I'll always remember seeing those pints of blood stored, waiting for survivors. It was an eye opening experience.

∞

My musical experience was useful the first year Clint was our host. Music would be with us throughout the event. Clint wanted to open the show with a lively number, and we agreed that some Broadway performers would entertain between fashion segments. Tracy Rosten, who was an old high school friend and had appeared with Tommy Tune in *Bye Bye Birdie*, would sing as well as Tommy Michaels (Timmy on *All My Children*) who had starred in *Les Miserables*. I was also able to enlist two other friends— Lauri Landry and David Jordan who had both toured in Broadway shows to sing a duet. This new aspect would allow me to do less fashion, but I had to rely more on other people to put together their musical segments. We also needed a piano and a sound system. *What did a sound system cost?*

These details had to be worked out with the catering liaison from the Marriott. Each additional feature to the show created new expenses. Although discounted for charity, it was still a fee that took away from the "bottom line," as they say, and would mean raising ticket prices and getting more enticing raffle and auction prizes.

That year the fashion lineup was exceptional. The young talent all came out. Kelly Ripa, who had just started as Hayley on *All My Children*, was as funny and clever as she is on *Live! with Kelly* today. She was also naturally pretty and easy to talk to. I remember she said, "Whatever you need, I'll do it." She even thanked me for inviting her.

Laura Sisk (who recently won an Emmy on *General Hospital* and is now Laura Wright) also modeled with Jessica Collins from *Loving*. They were both tall and exquisite looking with long blonde hair. I put them in Victorian shawls, over long dresses and flattering lacey skirts—they were beautiful. Tonya Walker participated again, and I think this time, she was more used to our designs. It was easier to find the right outfits for her. She brought Thom Christopher along, who was playing Carlo Hesser on *One Life To Live* at the time, and the two of them walked the runway together.

One of the people that stood out from that year was Michael Weatherly. He had just started on *Loving*, and I think that was his first daytime job. We did not know he was coming until he arrived, so we had to scurry to find him something to wear. I recall that he accommodated us and said, "Whatever you give me is fine."

He had chiseled fine features, blond hair, and sometimes he wore glasses, which really did not take away from how handsome he was. I told him to just go out on the runway and have a good time. I always told everyone where to walk to on the stage, which was set up like a T, and to come back quickly, turn to the audience, and smile before exiting. I should have timed this all out, but we never could get everyone together to do a "run through" so we just had to hope we finished before 11:00 p.m. at night when we would be charged for overtime.

Bob and Loyita Woods were the honorary chairs, and my friend Ilene, who was like a sister to me, volunteered to be the event chair. She and her then husband Abbey and his children were like an extended family to me. I welcomed whatever support she could bring as well as the aid of my brother Joel and sister-in-law Edie.

Ilene was very close to my mom and dad, and she often sat with them at the events. That year, I made her come on stage at the end and thank everyone. I also brought Meaghan Schick, and Clint introduced her while everyone applauded. It was then that Clint concluded the night by singing "Somewhere" from *West Side Story* (at my request). I thought that song would be mellow with inspiring lyrics to end the night. It left everyone feeling hopeful and proud to have been a part of the fundraiser. Kelly Ripa even had tears in her eyes.

Michael Weatherly, Laura Sisk,
Christopher Cousins, & Jessica Collins

That same year, I was asked to do a radio-thon to raise money for leukemia research. I have no idea what studio I went to, but I remember being impressed. The LLS wanted me to go on air and talk about my event, the fashions, and the celebrities who helped out and urge people to donate money. I had never spoken on the radio before. I had done television interviews, which petrified me, but usually with other people. This time, I would talk by myself—everyone said it would be like talking in my house because the interviewer would make me feel comfortable. Then I would go into another room and answer phone calls from people who were pledging money. I almost did not go—but I made it.

The nice thing about that day was that Michael Weatherly had also agreed to come on, and we sat in the green room together before going on. Our segments were separate, but knowing he was there made it easier for me to talk.

At the time, Michael was looking through the newspaper for an apartment to rent in Manhattan. I tried to give him some ideas about neighborhoods in New York since I had lived in almost all of them: Uptown, Downtown, Eastside, Westside, and Midtown. I did not want to be too pushy, but I was able to give him an idea of the kinds of advantages and disadvantages each one had. I was also a little star struck by him because I still was, underneath it all, a soap fan as I am to this day.

○8

Just to share with you how life comes full circle, I will tell you that I reconnected with Michael again this past year. When I had my Marriott shop, I met a wonderful woman named Harriet who could have been Elizabeth Taylor's double. She has become one of our dearest clients and friends. Harriet lives in California and used to come to New York to see Broadway shows and spend time with friends. She always stayed at the Marriott and hung out with us when she wasn't with her friends. We went to dinner together and she even met my family. One New Year's Eve we spent drinking, laughing, and partying while the almost inebriated guests came in and wished us all Happy New Year and bought some goodies to take home. Avé and I stayed over those nights and we had great

Avé and Jane

fun.

The Marriott New Year's Eve parties, right in the heart of everything, were the places to be. At midnight, guests could watch the ball drop from either their rooms or the 8th floor windows overlooking Times Square. The confetti came, people screamed, yelled, cried—everything—and then came into the shop. By the time we went to bed, it was almost time to open again. And Harriet shared some of those nights.

In California, Harriet worked on TV shows. She donated wonderful prizes for our event from the very popular *JAG* while it was on. The past few years she has been working on one of the most popular TV shows on CBS—*NCIS*. When I went to Los Angeles for the *Romantic Times Magazine* Convention in 2011, Harriet invited us to come to the set and say hello to Michael Weatherly who is now a huge TV star as DiNozzo on that show. I did not think he would remember me, but he truly did. He greeted us *so* warmly and said, "Of course, I remember you. You're not forgettable."

That was such a nice thing to say, and even though he only had a short time to visit with us, he showed me that he is still as unassuming, classy, and as gorgeous as he was when we knew him almost twenty years ago. Harriet made it very easy for us to visit that day, and we got to eat lunch with the cast and crew. Even her boss Charles Floyd Johnson welcomed us.

Ave, Michael Weatherly and Jane

Kerr Smith, an actor who appeared on *Dawson's Creek* and had participated in our fashion show when he was in New York, was a guest star and also remembered me. He was another dark-haired, good-looking young man then, and I remember him as very intelligent. He took time to talk to us and pose for pictures, as well. We even got to meet Mark Harmon who gave us time for a picture before he had to do an interview for *TV Guide*. He seemed very smart, handsome, and serious. I hold an enormous respect for him and the others in the show.

I thanked Harriet over and over again for all of us (Perry, Avé, Sue Coflin our photographer, and myself). The experience of being on a set and eating in the area where the crew and cast ate was priceless. How many people in their lifetime get to experience that? Not the celebrity of it, but the camaraderie I felt—they remembered me; they asked about the charity work; and they took the time to welcome us. Often celebrities seem so untouchable, but these people were sincerely interested in our lives. I have since sent all of them thank you notes and for their wives a little something from Jane Elissa Designs. I wanted them to know how special *they* are. I also know Harriet will support our charity efforts in the future, and I truly do love her as my friend.

With Clint Came Music

Clint stayed on as our host for the next year, and we were able to sustain the energy from the previous years. The committee grew and we now had Ilene as our chair, and her daughter-in-law Rosana Butler as our ticket selling chair. Bob and Loyita were being recognized for their contributions over the years, and my mother along with Walt presented them this new honor. More people were calling to attend. Rita Salk recruited the soap stars, and Broadway singers were beginning to hear about the event. It seemed as if we were going forward in the right direction, but we still had to tighten the show.

There were so many people backstage that year. Barbara Beroff continued to work with Avé on lining all the models up and sending them out on cue. Pat Sellers, who wrote for *Soap Weekly* and was often pulling her gorgeous red hair out of her head as we changed the lineup, was still our fashion commentator. A young Sarah Michelle Geller, new to *All My Children*, participated and so did Sydney Penny from the same show. Her character's name was Julia, and I remembered her as a young actress in the *Thorn Birds*. Both of them came to the shop for fittings and looked absolutely charming in some of our 1920s clothes. Something Sarah Michelle did stuck in my mind—she wanted a piece of jewelry from the shop, but she did not have money that day. I told her to take it. She insisted she wanted to pay for it, and I said it was not necessary. A few days after the fashion show, I received a thank you letter and a check for the price of the jewelry. Sarah Michelle was a class act.

Valarie Pettiford from *One Life To Live* sang that year as did Laurie Beechman. Valarie went on to star in *Fosse* on Broadway and work in California in television. She and I have remained in contact, and she recently came to my apartment to do a photo shoot for my "Hats for Health" business. She also is a fan of my art and purchased a New York scene painting which hangs in her Los Angeles home. I consider it an honor to call her my friend.

There were so many other participants that year—Catherine joined us again. Her husband, Michael Knight, Tad from *All My Children,* came to watch. *Young and the Restless* star Michael Damian who was performing in *Joseph and the Amazing Technicolor Dream Coat* on Broadway came to support Catherine as well. Susan Diol brought her friend Shaun Cassidy, who was appearing in *Blood Brothers* on Broadway and was able to stop by before the show. He actually met my mother and posed for pictures. I remember thinking what a big star he was and how unassuming. Casper Van Dien, new to One Life to Live, came out with his shirt open and thrilled the fans. Later, he married Carrie Mitchum and went to Hollywood to star in movies.

Sarah Michelle Geller, Casper Van Dien, & Sydney Penny

Windsor Harmon was another fresh face on *All My Children*, and he thrilled the fans when he came out shirtless with only a tie and blue jeans. He is now on *The Bold and Beautiful*. Brian L. Green and Sandra Reinhardt were also two of my favorite models as they always knew how to have fun on the runway and entertain the fans. There were many, many more stars, and it seemed to be a long night, but the fans loved it.

I sent thank you notes to everyone, especially Clint Holmes and Bob and Loyita Woods. Without them the event would never have evolved as it did. They were people who were committed to helping me make something grow, and I wanted them to know how deeply that moved me. I also wanted to tell them that we had raised a significant amount of money, and I hoped to continue doing that.

I was beginning to understand that my life had taken a new direction. There were celebrity meetings, studio visits, magazine photos, and suddenly an entree into the backstage world of the acting profession. For some reason, the birth of this new adventure took my mind back to my early life. Memories of Brooklyn floated through my head.

Memories of Brooklyn

$\mathcal{M}$y memories of Brooklyn and the early days with my cousins are precious to me. My Aunt Lil and Uncle Henry were the closest family I had beyond my parents and siblings. Lillian was always excited to see me, and she would grab me and say "Jaaaaaaanie" forever. Henry was a little less approachable, but he smiled at me when our family came to visit. Lillian had the most enormous brown eyes and they were *always* made up. They seemed to have a sense of wonderment about them, which engulfed me, so I listened intently every time she spoke.

Henry would go off with my dad into the living room and play cards or watch television. I was expected to sit in the kitchen with my mom, aunt, and grandma, but I never wanted to do that. I wanted to be with the boys—my male cousins and my brother Joel. I would sneak away and go into the living room to watch sports or learn how to play pinochle.

My cousins Arnie and Mike were older, and I adored and admired them. My brother, who was younger, followed everyone also. Of course, Arnie, being the oldest, was our leader, and I would just sit and listen to whatever he said. From an early age, we were told how smart he was, and I really believed he was a genius. At the age of four, he even walked around saying "me boss, me boss" to everyone. He was opinionated, verbal, and could talk endlessly. The grownups said to listen to him, so I did.

I know I had an idealized image of Arnie, but in truth, he was very quixotic. He *was* brilliant. He graduated top of his class in high school (Erasmus High School in Brooklyn which Barbara Streisand attended at that time), won a Westinghouse Scholarship, and was the first of us to go to college—Harvard, of course.

When he sent me a Harvard sweatshirt, I wore it all the time to show off. At Harvard, he was also in the top of his class, and upon graduation, got a prime job at IBM. I dreamed he would change the world, discover a cure for cancer, or be President. There was nothing I thought he couldn't do. But there sometimes is another side to brilliance, and for all the positive things he could do, there was something in him that took him outside the box, as they say. He rebelled in life, and the strict dress code at IBM did not suit him. He left that company very quickly—his life took many twists and turns and to this day, I have never understood some of his choices, but he always communicated with and advised me well.

I remember, when I was in college, I was having difficulty adjusting and wrote him long letters. I did not understand or know myself well. Arnie wrote me a letter I still have today, which touched me deeply. He talked about his own insecurities and uncertainties and how he had tried to find a place for his restless soul. He called me after the letter, and we had an hour long conversation about getting to know and accept yourself. It was a rare moment between us because Arnie always had such an outward bravado that, up until that time, I never realized the burden he carried, to always be expected to be smart, clever, and witty. It was more than I could have handled, and I think too much for him.

His younger brother Michael was closer to my age, and I spent many hours talking with him. He was quieter and less showy than Arnie, but also very intelligent. We would go to the park together with the family, and I remember hanging on to Michael as my protector. Everyone would laugh at me as I tried to fit in, but I didn't mind. I enjoyed being the *only* girl.

I also enjoyed spending time in my grandparents' apartment. It was downstairs in my aunt's building. Grandma always greeted me with home-baked cookies, and Grandpa gave me lots of pennies. I thought Grandpa was some kind of pirate because he came here on a ship from South Africa without telling any of his family. My grandmother, on the other hand, was more of an earth mother, and she taught me how to cook, crochet, knit and sew. She decorated her small sofa with handmade doilies and embroidered pillows. I remember all the white lace aprons and the placemats she made, and I wanted to be just like her. I would climb on Grandpa's knee and try to hold a crochet needle (which would fall out of my hand) and make a doily. I think my desire to sew things was born right in their living room.

My grandfather took me on my first carousel ride in Prospect Park. When I saw the carousel, all I could see were candy stripes and colors—red, yellow, black and white—an array of wonder—brown manes, white horses, balloons, children running everywhere. Everyone rushed to get on a pony and I ran, too. Grandpa had to help me on to the little horse, but once I was on, I never wanted to get off. As we went round and round, I turned to look back at him and he waved. His eyes were crinkling, and I even thought I saw him laugh at me. It was a special moment—indelible in my memory.

From there he took me to a world of alluring, sweet smells I had never experienced before. He wanted to show me the Brooklyn Botanic Gardens—rows and rows of magnificent flowers and swarms of colors—irregular patterns and shapes—curves, circles and points—pinks, lilacs, fuchsias, aquas—I was in heaven. Even then I knew I loved colors and patterns. I wanted to grab them all and take them home, but Grandpa said, "No." I could only look.

"But I want to keep the picture forever, Grandpa," I remember saying.

And he said, "You will. Whenever you close your eyes, you will be able to see those flowers again. Just keep it in your mind and it will be there."

I didn't believe him then, but he was right—when I want to see gardens and floral patterns in fabrics, I envision those gardens in Brooklyn and a warmth envelopes my body. How precious that day was, and how true it is that it never ended. Somehow I saw my shop as an extension of that beautiful garden.

The Window/Julie Harris

I strived to establish my store to reflect the unique aspects of the New York experience. I learned quickly that tourists enjoyed seeing New York celebrities and landmarks. We displayed photos from my events around the store, and people would ask if we really knew famous people. Since I was not in the store a lot, our manager would explain who I was and who the people were. In time we had such a collection that I created what I jokingly called "the wall of shame." It was on the right side of the store as customers walked in, and people from all over the world would stop and stare. It brought them into the shop, and eventually, many came to our events. They also admired our merchandise. Between the whimsical window and the photos, we were able to entice people to purchase merchandise and increase revenue.

The Marriott was the premier Broadway hotel at the time. Actors from shows frequently came to the lounge after matinees and many of them visited our store. On a Sunday afternoon, my eighteen-year-old intern, Rosa, was in charge while I did some designing at my studio. I was engrossed in painting a jacket when the phone rang.

It was Rosa. "There's a Miss Harris here, and she wants to buy some things, but she wants to pay by check. What do I do?" She knew that we did not take checks as we had difficulties with bounced ones in the past.

"Does she have a credit card?" I asked.

I could hear Rosa talking to her. "Not with her. She just came by from rehearsals for a show and all she has is her checkbook."

"What is her name?" I asked.

"Miss Harris," Rosa replied.

Miss Harris, I mused to myself. Miss Harris—I kept thinking of who it might be. Then it came to me. Could this be the legendary Julie Harris who had appeared with James Dean in the movie *East of Eden*—the famous movie and stage actress? "Rosa," I said. "Do you know who she is? Is she Julie Harris?"

Never had it crossed my mind that a high school senior from the Bronx would not know Julie Harris—but it was another generation, and to my surprise, she did not.

"Yes. Her name is Julie Harris."

"Put her on please."

I apologized to her for Rosa not recognizing her, and I gushed on the phone about being a *super* fan. She was so soft spoken and pleasant and although she did not have her credit card, she loved our merchandise and wanted to purchase Jane Elissa designs for gifts and for herself. I told Rosa to take her check, which had her address and phone number on it, and when she left, I explained to Rosa who she was. Rosa remained unfazed, but talking to Miss Harris had made my day, and the fact that she would wear our berets and give shawls and other things as gifts was thrilling.

Although she was unable to attend our Leukemia Extravaganza, she generously brought signed books she had written to the shop and donated them to our auction. She also personally signed one to me which I still appreciate.

The Board/Loraine

As I built my retail business at the Marriott, I was also becoming even more involved with fundraising. The Leukemia Society office became very familiar to me. The New York City chapter of the LLS had a volunteer Board of Directors. I was not sure exactly what these people did, but I felt it was an honor to be a part of the organization. Susan, the executive director at the time, asked me if I would like to join. It would require going to meetings once a month and committing to continue to work on my events. I would learn about the advances in leukemia and be invited to meet some of the sponsored researchers. I would also have the opportunity to meet board members who might wish to get involved with my event, and it would expand my visibility within the organization. I was not too familiar with how the LLS worked and being a "trustee" would allow me full access to information about the national organization. It was a commitment, however, and I did not know if I had the time to give outside of my business obligations. I had to think about it.

Again, new people. Again, new responsibilities. Again, more commitment, more visibility, more opportunity—

Ah-ha! Try to think of this as a positive thing. "It will be an honor," I told myself. It was another step coming from that first phone call to the society.

CR

The first board meeting was held in Midtown at PricewaterhouseCoopers, the office of the Board President. The closest I had ever come to dealing with accounting firms was when I worked for a year in a totally miscast role as an administrative assistant. It was a job I had found through my CPA friend Ilene, and they hired me to do temp work for the summer. They later asked me to stay for a year to cover for an assistant who was on medical leave. I did, but when a teaching job came up, I took it. I needed to get back to my artistic side.

I signed in and went to one of the highest floors in the building, which housed the boardroom. I buzzed in and a volunteer from the LLS escorted me into the room. Everyone was already there, and they just stared at me: 90 percent men in suits and ties, the LLS executive director, a female secretary to take notes, and one other woman sitting across from me. I was introduced and had to speak briefly about my event, and then the meeting began.

I was so intimidated! The room was larger than my whole apartment. The mahogany conference table could have filled my living room. The ceiling was twenty feet high, and the room had what appeared to be more books than a library. I felt overwhelmed. I just took out a notebook and wrote things down. I have no idea what anyone said that day because I was busy trying to figure out who these people were and my role among them.

After the meeting ended, I approached the only other female member in the group and officially introduced myself. Her name was Loraine Jacobs, and she had been married to Jimmy Jacobs who died of leukemia. He had been a champion handball player and then a manager for an up and coming boxer named Mike Tyson. She was a petite woman with beautiful brown eyes and brown hair. Her manner was engaging, and I immediately felt comfortable with her. She said she had heard about my events and would love to learn more about them. I told her I was very nervous, and she smiled saying, "Don't let them fool you. We are all here for the same cause and some of them might even enjoy your event."

We exchanged numbers and walked out together. Without Loraine on the board, I do not think I would have gotten through those first two years. Later, I was able to have some members model in my fashion show, but it took a while for me to be comfortable. I learned how to interact on a professional level with the other board members, but it did not come easily.

Bidding

One of the perks of my new life was that I was invited to attend other activities sponsored by the Leukemia Society throughout the year. I often donated Jane Elissa designs to the auctions at such fundraisers. Although I could not afford the top tickets, I was able to purchase less expensive ones and attend many galas. My fellow board member, Loraine Jacobs, usually purchased tickets, as well, and I loved to sit with her. If it was a sporting event, Ernie would come, and if it was a theater event, Annie Albarian liked to go. All in all, just being a part of the Leukemia Board brought me great pleasure.

One of my favorite evenings was a Young Professional Society Ties and Blackjack Event. It featured a casino atmosphere with food, gambling or prizes, and dancing. Ernie and I loved it. Even though we didn't gamble, we enjoyed dancing and the venue was very free spirited and festive. I helped find the DJ one year, and the place was filled with Rock and Roll and Disco. We danced almost every dance until we decided to eat the delicious food. But the best part of the night for me was the silent auction. The prizes there were fabulous. They were often sports related, and since Ernie and I loved sports, I bid for many of the prizes.

The first year I went, I had major competition from a fellow board member and friend Jon. He was a young, single—tall, dark and handsome—Wall Street trader, and at that time he had money to burn. The problem was he always bid against me, and even if I pushed myself, I could not meet his final bids. So year after year I lost out. Finally, for whatever reason, he was unable to attend. *Yes*, it was my chance. I bid on everything I wanted—an ESPN poster signed from the ESPY awards by tons of sports and TV personalities, a Mike Tyson fight jacket from Las Vegas, but the best was the opportunity to be an extra on one of my favorite shows, *Law & Order*. What a treat that would be if I could get it. It would be the fulfillment of a lifelong dream to be in the background on a TV show.

Of course, there were other people bidding, and a half hour before the bidding ended, I hovered around all the silent auction sheets. Ernie stood at one post, and I waited at the other. The sports poster was expensive—over nine hundred dollars—but I told Ernie I wanted it, so he kept bidding. The Tyson jacket was also high, but the *Law & Order* walk-on was trouble—fifteen hundred with ten minutes left. I stayed glued to the spot, pen in hand, ready to pounce.

...Someone was walking up. Oh no, they grabbed a pen—$1600. I smiled with two minutes left—$1,700 I wrote. It was a handsome young man, probably another Wall Street trader. He smiled. I smiled. He didn't write, but the pen remained in his hand. Two minutes to go. Both of us still smiling, still standing. He put his pen down, $1,800. He looked at me with that same smile, only it seemed bigger. I just sighed and shook my head. How much higher could I go? It was for a good cause, but I had already given so much that year. Could I go any higher? Again, I shook my head, shrugged my shoulders, and pretended to walk away. He seemed satisfied and turned his back, thirty seconds, twenty seconds, ten seconds—$2,000 I wrote. Just as he turned back, they announced the auction was over.

"Yippee," I shrieked.

He stared at me as if I were crazy. I showed him my bid.

"No" he said, shaking his head. "I don't believe it. When did you write that?"

I grinned the grin of a Cheshire cat and said, "When you

weren't looking."

I was ecstatic. This was something I was going to remember my whole life. A trip to *Law & Order*. Maybe I would meet Jerry Orbach, who I had adored since I saw the play *Carnival* as a young girl. Or I might see Sam Waterston or maybe even talk to the producer about getting an extra walk-on slot for my benefit. Air couldn't hold me. I ran to Ernie and he told me we had won the other prizes, too. Five thousand dollars later, we collected our winnings and left. It was an expensive night, but the beginning of a new journey. What could top that?

Broadway Cares

*W*hat topped it was another auction. As part of my fundraising endeavors, I met people from another organization named Broadway Cares Equity Fights AIDS. When we first opened our shop, a very handsome Broadway aficionado named John Fahey came in and asked me if I would put their poster in the window. The poster was advertising a "flea market" in Shubert Alley to raise money for BCEFA. The organization was formed to help people who contracted AIDS. At that time, not much was known about the disease, and it seemed to be ravaging the Broadway community. I agreed to put the poster in the window and offered to donate one of our Broadway jackets to the auction. John said he'd get back to me on that; I displayed the poster, and that was the beginning of my relationship with BCEFA. Over the years, I have contributed to and attended many of their events. I put their poster in my shop and encouraged people who did not understand about AIDS to become more knowledgeable and compassionate to the people who were affected by this horrible illness. It was important for me to be supportive because I knew many friends in the theater who had lost companions or fellow performers to the disease. It was like a cancer in the theater community.

One year my friend, Pat Sellers, went to the flea market and bid on a walk-on part in a Broadway show. The show was *Will Rogers' Follies*, and she invited Ernie and me to come and see her.

She had discounted tickets, and we sat in the fifth row with a whole group of her friends. Pat, with her flaming red hair, was easy to pick out on stage. She wore a cowgirl outfit in most of her scenes, and all I remember was her smiling and giggling whenever she was on stage. They put her name in the program, and she took a special bow. I was *so* envious as this had been one of my fantasies growing up. I had always wanted to be on stage—not as the star—but in the ensemble. If she could do it, why not me? When would be my chance?

The next year BCEFA had another flea market and an auction. The weather was cloudy and rather windy, but my mind was set on being there. I didn't care if I had to close my shop for two hours, I would attend that auction. It was my year! At 5:00 p.m. Jenelle, my intern came, and I met Pat at the auction. She had the list of items and one of the walk-ons was for *Guys and Dolls*. I had always loved that show and had seen it staring Peter Gallagher, Faith Prince, and Nathan Lane. They were no longer in it, but it didn't matter. I just wanted to be on stage. There were fewer people than the year before, but the bidding was still spirited. Package after package went, and I waited patiently for the walk-ons. Pat monitored how much everything was going for, and the amounts were still very high. My nerves kicked in because I knew my bidding limit, and I did not want to get carried away as I had at some leukemia functions. But I *really* wanted this.

The announcement came: "And now we have a once in a lifetime priceless opportunity to appear on Broadway."

The crowd moved to push in—an opening bid was called for—the bidding began—six hundred—seven—eight—on and on, different people called out. When it was at fifteen hundred—all went quiet. My hand shot up. "Sixteen hundred," I said.

Since I hadn't bid before, everyone seemed to turn and look at me. Pat was laughing. "You're on kid."

"Seventeen hundred dollars," someone else offered. Eighteen hundred, nineteen—quiet again.

"Going once."

"Two thousand," I shouted.

Then it was really quiet. It was down to me and another lady.

The auctioneer held up his hand with a grin. "I just got word that if you will match the two thousand, I can give you both a walk-on."

The other lady looked as if she would cry. "Yes," she screamed.

And it was done. We both had walk-ons. I was going to be on Broadway in *Guys and Dolls. No way!*

Law & Order

The night before I was to go to the set of *Law & Order*, I had a mild panic attack. Although I had been interviewed on television before, I had never actually prepared to be part of a television show. There was a process I had to go through once my bid was accepted. First, I had to call the casting agency, Sylvia Faye. The man there instructed me to send full body photos of myself, a head shot, and a description—age, skin color, height, weight, hair and eye color, measurements, etc. He explained that they needed to see what I looked like to determine which episode of *Law & Order* and where in that show they could fit me. I would be considered an extra and had to come to the office to fill out the necessary forms for a job application, and I would receive "extra pay" for that day. I told him I had made a charitable donation and did not expect to be paid, but he said that was how it worked.

"Okay," I said. "Whatever I'm supposed to do I will do."

I gathered up all the photos I had, wrote a description of myself, and went to the office two days later. It was a small office with piles of photos on desks and walls covered with celebrities. I was amazed at how many nighttime television stars had apparently been hired by Sylvia Faye. I didn't really know anything about a casting agency, but their job is to find background people for the New York shows. If you wanted to be on a show as an actor or actress, you needed to either have an agent represent you, or send your photos to an agency, which decided if you were right for any shows. Sometimes they wanted a certain type to stand out and other times they were just looking for average people to fit into the background. *Average* meant people who did not have any outstanding features, large nose, big eyes, big hair, etc., so their looks would not distract from the stars of the show. The purpose of being an extra was to blend in. Since I consider myself a regular-looking person, I thought I wouldn't have trouble being in the background.

When I walked into the casting room and met the man who would place me, he said, "Oh, you are Jane; you are not quite what I expected."

"Why?" I asked.

"You stand out," was his reply.

I did not know if that was good or bad.

"You have beautiful, long red hair. Smile for me, please."

I smiled.

"Did you ever want to be an actress?" he asked.

I said, "At one time I wanted to sing on stage."

"Well, if you ever want to work, let me know. If you could act a little, I probably could get you some under five lines, or even some small roles. You have a certain look."

I stared at him. Was he joking? I had never really taken notice of my look before as it frequently changed. Being an artist, I always experimented with clothes. Although my hair is red now, it is not my natural color. I had grown up as a pale-skinned, hazel-eyed, black-haired girl, which was unusual. Most dark-haired girls were not as fair as I was, and I hated it because I always thought I seemed ashy. As I got older, I adjusted to it, but I still would never own a tan. I would become burnt red and that was not pleasant. Besides looking like a fried lobster, I had to endure the flaking and peeling. I looked like I had psoriasis. It never ended in the summer because I didn't tan––I would continue to burn. Pretty soon I hid under umbrellas and tried to avoid the sun. That was even worse because then I was the only pale person in a teenage world of tan bathing beauties. This embarrassed me, but *much later* in life I learned to accept my differences. I also began dying my hair red in my late twenties as a premature silver gray was sneaking in. Once I did that, I finally felt comfortable with my pale skin. My eyes seemed greener, my complexion seemed to have a glow, and people would stop me on the street and tell me what beautiful hair I had. I started to develop a little more confidence in my appearance. It came late in life, but it was a nice change from growing up totally insecure about my looks. So I took his comments as a compliment and moved on.

"We have a spot in the next *Law & Order*," he was saying. "The director will place you. You will get a call a few days before telling you where to report and what time and what to wear. Good luck!" He put out his hand, smiled slightly, and said good-bye. On to the next starstruck hopeful.

True to his word, in less than a week I received a call from the production office at *Law & Order*. "Ms. Jane Meyers, please."

"That's me," I replied.

"Are you available to report at 6:00 a.m. on Thursday to our Chelsea Studio Piers for extra work on *Law & Order*? Please come early as there is some paperwork you must fill out and the day may run long so bring something to do while you are waiting for your part. Bring two different outfits as well. You will be sitting in the spectator section of the courtroom and the director will place you. Any questions? Oh, and you must do your own hair and makeup, so be prepared."

A pause.

"That's fine," I said. "I'll be there."

"Okay, we'll see you then."

The call came on a Tuesday to report on Thursday. That gave me two days to be nervous. I kept thinking about the initial call I had made to the Leukemia Society and how many things had changed in my life once again. When I made the call, I never thought I would be living out some of my childhood fantasies. I was going to be in a prime time television series even though it was only as an extra. What would it be like to be on a set? Where did everyone wait to be called, and what would they think of me?

How would they treat me? It was going to be quite a day.

I checked in at 5:45 a.m. The people at the desk told me to go to the extra room and sign in there. They also told me to be sure to tell the person I was seeing that I was one of the charity bidders as they were prepared for me. I didn't know what that meant, but I followed instructions like a robot. Go here, sign this, sit there and wait. I filled out more papers so I would be paid, and then went to wait with the others and have some breakfast.

The room he had directed me to was filled with people. It seemed like there were at least thirty people in fifty square feet. It was crowded and dank. There were no windows and the walls were painted a fading beige. There were two large tables covered with mini bagels, mini muffins, and some spreads. I assumed this was breakfast. I looked again at the room and realized there were not enough chairs for everyone. I grabbed the first chair I saw, and put my little suitcase and purse on top. I was not going to stand for whatever length of time it took to get called. The people in the room looked very much like me. They were the extras group. Everyone seemed to know each other, and people were talking about the different shows they had acted in.

One woman had a whole book of pictures and credits and kept going up to the person who had signed us in to show him the book and remind him of all her work. I didn't really know why she was doing this, but I learned later that she was attempting to get a better spot in the extra pool. I learned that some of the extras just blended in and were never seen by the viewer. But others, depending upon the angle of the camera, might be seen many times. If an extra was seen, it gave them more leverage in negotiating a better spot on the next job, and if a casting director noticed someone, he might want to offer them a bigger part in an ensuing project. It was a very singularly focused room. Everyone wanted to be noticed, except me, of course. I just sat there watching and listening.

What fascinated me most about the room was the fact that everyone took themselves so seriously, and they were all actors. They all thought of themselves that way and went from show to show hoping for a big break to get an under five speaking part so they could join the union and get paid more. I learned all this from a very beautiful young woman sitting next to me who liked the hat I was wearing. Of course, it was one of my designs, but it was a rather simple one, all grays, black, and whites with a small brim. I thought no one would notice. She kept talking about how great I would fit in on some movie she had worked on. I smiled and explained I was not usually an extra although I was thrilled to be there to learn about the backstage world of television. She told me each show was different, but *Law & Order* was pretty typical of the New York shows. You ate a little, waited a lot, did your time on set, and went home. You never mingled with the stars. That was the hierarchy. The stars had their own room. They ate separately; they had hair and makeup calls, and you never talked to them on set. Those were the rules. We sat there for three hours before someone finally came to select people for the different scenes.

Someone had just phoned the production assistant to tell him he was going to be late, and I heard her say, "You have been replaced. You have done this too many times and that's it."

So someone from the extra pool was going to be elevated. I think the person chosen was a little above an ordinary extra and knew he might be needed. The actor had brought enough clothes for his new role and was very prepared. The production assistant handed him a script and the actor said, "Don't worry, I'm ready." He was then taken to another room and I never saw him again.

Everyone else was choosing their outfits, and someone called my name and another man's name. "Come with me please and bring your things."

I looked around. The other man was young and smiling. He was dressed in a beautiful suit and talked a lot more than I did. He had also bid on this opportunity at a different function. We were now going to be introduced to the director. We were greeted warmly by members of the staff and told how appreciative the charities were for our donation. They told me to wear exactly what I was wearing, a fairly nondescript suit. (I had remembered I must blend in.) We were then informed that we would be reporters in the courtroom. We were given steno books to actually look like we were writing for a newspaper or magazine. I felt a lot more comfortable knowing I would be sitting, rather than standing. It seemed easy enough.

We went back to the extra room, put our belongings down, and were told to stand in front of a lining-up extra group. We were marched like school kids quietly into the anteroom before the courtroom set. Then the other charity bidder and I were called to the front of the line. The production assistant whispered something to a girl who was seating everyone, and placed us in the spectators' booth. The male bidder was seated first on the left side, and I was on the right. I would be behind two major characters in the story, and the camera would cut to them a lot during the trial. It was a good seat because I would be seen on camera frequently. I thanked her and she said it was important for me to be seen since I had spent a lot of money for the opportunity. I smiled.

She then sat all the other extras. No one said a word about their placement. I'm sure some of them wanted to be in more visible places, but they never said anything. They were still part of the show no matter where they ended up and that was all that was important.

Other people came in and out during the sound and lighting checks, but they were not featured actors, they were stand-ins. They did all the waiting while everything was adjusted. It took about forty-five minutes, and I doodled in my steno pad. When everything was ready, the main actors appeared for a few moments to do a double check, and that was it. We were about to begin. Now I was nervous. Was my lipstick on? Was my hair straight? Should I smile? How should I act? We were told to be reporters and be interested in the trial but not to fidget or move around. Just sit there like props. That's how I felt, like part of the scenery.

The actors were speaking. Sam Waterston was saying his lines. I sat behind David McCallum. I could not believe it. I thought he was so cute in *The Man from UNCLE*, and I had watched him on television. Now, I was right behind him. My God, he was a guest star, so every time the camera took his picture, I would be seen. Then Sam was talking again, the lady on the witness stand muffed a line.... Break, shoot again. Start from the beginning.... Lines were correct that time. Camera moving around, was I in the picture? I could never tell which direction the camera was coming from. I hadn't known that they shot scenes from different angles with so many cameras. I didn't even know if I was in camera range. I would just have to wait to see the show.

Finally, the scene was done. We had to wait for the stars to leave, and then we were escorted back to our room. I was tired, not physically, but emotionally. I hadn't seen Jerry Orbach, and I found out he was not on set that day. I did, however, get an opportunity to meet Sam Waterston. Everyone was told there would be a break, and we could leave as the remaining shooting schedule for that day did not include the extras. Thank goodness because it was only around 2:00 p.m. giving me time to accomplish many more things that day.

As I was packing, the Production Assistant came over to me and asked me if I would like a tour of the rest of the sets. I said absolutely, and she took me into the interrogation room, the jail, and back into the courtroom. She explained to me how the cameras worked and why it took so long to set things up. All the preparation had to be done before extras could even come on the set. The actors had to know their places so there were things called marks, where they would stand. It was like a choreographed ballet. Every move was pre-planned. If the lighting wasn't right on that spot, things had to be adjusted.

When the tour was over, she said she was sorry that Jerry Orbach wasn't there, but this was the courtroom part, and in that episode, the police were not involved. Sam Waterston was in hair and makeup, and if I wanted to say a short hello, she would bring me in. I said, of course, and we went into the mirrored room while he was in the chair. It looked like a barber chair, and he had a small apron-type cloth covering his clothes. I was interrupting his time, but he turned and offered me his hand. I shook it and told him that I loved the show, and how much I enjoyed his acting. He smiled and thanked me and also told me what a generous thing it was for me to bid to be on the show. I thanked him and said I'll be watching.

"Good luck," he replied and that was it. My day was complete.

Broadway

After I paid for my Broadway package, I received an envelope with the instructions for how to proceed with my debut. I called the number for the production office the very next day (A little over anxious, wouldn't you say?), and they told me to call back the following Tuesday. I asked if I needed to do anything before I called (like send pictures or describe myself), and they said no. Someone would explain everything when I called back.

The next week couldn't come fast enough. I was going to live my dream. I would be on a Broadway stage. I wouldn't even have to sing. I could blend right in with the scenery, but I would still be there. I *would* be there. What if I made a mistake? It's not like TV where they could reshoot the scene—I could affect the flow of the show. I was really concerned. But that wouldn't happen, I assured myself. They'll prep me. I'll be "ready for my close up," as Norma Desmond used to say.

Tuesday came and I dialed the production office.

"No one is available. Please leave a message."

More waiting. It was 12:00 p.m. Where were they?

An hour later the phone rang and it was a lady with a sing-song voice. "Hello, is this Jane?"

"Yes, it is."

"I'm Laura from the Guys & Dolls Company, and I am going to be your guide through this process. Thank you for making that generous contribution to BCEFA. Could you be available to come and meet tomorrow between shows at the theater? I would like to show you around and introduce you to the wardrobe mistress. She will help you with costumes and help us determine which scene would work best for you."

"Yes, I can certainly meet you. Where do I go and at what time?"

"Be at the 45th Street stage door at 4:45 p.m. and I will meet you there. Just tell the guard you are there to see Laura."

"Okay, see you then," I said and hung up.

Tomorrow, so soon. How should I dress? Do I wear a suit or am I casual? Should I wear a "Jane Elissa" hat and jacket? Will I fit into this cast? I wasn't exactly svelte like most Broadway performers. What costume would be for me? So much to think about. I decided to dress casually, but I did wear a Jane Elissa hat. As usual, it was one of the first comments I received.

"I like your hat," said the guard.

It was a good way to start.

I waited for Laura, and when she came, she shook my hand quickly and said we did not have a lot of time because everyone had to get ready for the evening show and have their dinner. One of the assistant directors was on the stage with two actors giving them notes from the previous performance and changing a short dance segment.

"No dancing for me," I said.

Laura laughed. "No, for you very simple staging."

That made me happy. This was the first time I'd ever been on a Broadway stage, and it gave me a thrill. I hadn't yet touched the front of the stage, but just walking behind, seeing all the wires, scaffolding, and scenery was exciting. But I had no idea where I was headed.

The Broadway stage is just what we see, but underneath is a whole other world. There were two levels and the dressing rooms and wardrobe sections were below. I always imagined them to be behind but that was not so. They were either across the floor, as in the Minskoff Theater where *Scarlett Pimpernel* was playing, or below as with *Guys & Dolls*. The actors had to race up and down steps all the time. I realize what great shape they were in and vowed to watch my junk food intake at least until I finished my performance. I wanted to be able to go up and down without being breathless.

Laura took me through what seemed to be a maze of rooms. She showed me the hair and makeup area for the chorus. There were so many bright lights I could see every mark on my face. That did not please me. I would have to confront all my freckles, blemishes, and wrinkles. Laura must have guessed what I was thinking because she told me I would be professionally made up, and I would have stage makeup and probably a wig so I didn't have to worry about my appearance. The professionals would take care of everything. I asked about the wig, and she explained that *Guys & Dolls* was a period piece and most women had different hairdos than the ones we had now. Also, it was easier to keep everything in place with a wig. I hadn't known that in most shows the actors were wearing wigs. It was just part of their costume.

Then the time came for me to meet the wardrobe mistress Gloria and her assistant Sam. Gloria had curly hair with glasses on top of her head, and she wore a smock. She was in her late twenties and had been working on the show for two years. Her assistant Sam was younger, very thin and very energetic. He shook my hand enthusiastically and said, "Let's see what we can find for you."

Good-bye to Laura. "You're in good hands," she said. "Break a leg."

The wardrobe room was a large area filled with floor racks, ceiling racks, faux closets, etc. Each character had a section marked with their name. When they reported to work, they came to this room to get their costumes. After the show, the costumes were placed back in the character's section and either cleaned, pressed, or sewn depending on what had happened that night. Each star had a dresser to expedite quick changes. I could imagine that this large dressing area was an extremely hectic place before, during, and after the show. The job of wardrobe mistress would definitely *not be* for me.

Gloria and Sam explained that I would be playing different characters in background scenes. *Guys & Dolls* revolves around two gangsters and the two women they love. One of the gangsters is tall, dark, and handsome, and he falls in love with the lady who works at the Salvation Army. The other gangster is short, chubby, and humorous (think Nathan Lane on Broadway), and his girlfriend works in a nightclub. The different sets were switched rapidly during the play, and Sam thought I would have sufficient time to be in four scenes. I just looked at him and giggled. "Anything you say," I said.

"Okay. Here are the costumes. Let's see what size you might be."

Of course, most of the costumes were small, but there was an actress who was about my size (somewhere between a six and an eight), and Sam thought I could fit into her wardrobe without much alteration. I tried on the first two outfits, and they fit almost perfectly. Sam showed me that he had safety pins in the back of one dress which was a little large for me. This was the same trick we used when we put on fashion shows in the garment center. The public doesn't know that models are pinned together into their clothes as they walk down the runway. Nothing ever fits as perfectly as it does on the sample girl. It's all illusion.

The last two dresses did not need any changes so I was all set from that standpoint. I did, however, have to wear hose, shoes, jewelry, and other accessories. For each outfit, we talked about the possibility of how to present the full image of the character I was supposed to be.

My first scene was sitting at a nightclub table listening to music and watching singers perform. Sam said they put me at the first table so I could be seen clearly from the audience. I wasn't sure about that since it would be my first time on stage, and I thought it would be better for me to go right into the scenery.

"What do you mean?" he asked. "You paid all that money not to be seen? Are you crazy? You're going to be front and center."

Okay. That wasn't exactly what I wanted, but whatever they told me to do, I would do.

The second scene they said would be a cross. Sam continued, "And you'll wear this pink suit (shocking fuchsia) with this lovely pillbox hat. No one will miss you in that. You'll walk across the stage with the closed curtain talking to a gangster suitor while everyone behind the curtain sets up the next scene."

"You mean it's just me and my suitor, by ourselves, on stage all alone?"

"Yes," Sam said. "You're supposed to be out for an evening stroll in the moonlight. It will be fun. Then once your stroll is over, you can change quickly into this party dress, and in the second act, you can be at the nightclub again. Do you want to do a fourth change?"

"No," I said. I was already panicked enough. Where would I go to change? Who would take my costumes? Who would walk across the stage with me? Oh my God, this was getting to be more than I had imagined.

Sam must have looked at my face and seen the fear because he put his arm on my shoulders and said, "Don't worry, we will all be here for you. Everything will be fine."

I sighed deeply, and he wrote my name on my three costumes and put them in their place. I was now part of the cast.

"The next step," he said, "is to choose a wig. For that you will meet Charlene."

I went up the steps to another room, and Charlene appeared; tall, thin, angular and happy. Not a wrinkle on her face. "Hi there, I'm Charlene. I'm going to make you into a *doll*."

Really, I thought. You have a long way to go.

"Let's try on some wigs. I want you to have *big blonde hair*."

"But I don't look good as a blonde, I'm too pale," I said.

"You won't be pale when I finish with you. The stage lights require a lot of makeup, and you will be gorgeous."

She called Sam, and I guess they discussed my costumes because in five minutes Sam was at the door with the pink silk two-piece outfit and the hat I would wear for my cross.

"I'll leave it here," he explained to Charlene. "You can pick the wig to match this outfit as it will be the one she takes her bow in."

Bow—I hadn't even thought about that. Now is not the time. Too much to do.

"Here, Jane. I think this wig will be perfect."

"Are you sure, Charlene?" I was not used to so much hair.

"Just try it."

We rolled my long red hair into a little knot, put a skull cap on to hold it in place, and then put this very large wig on my head. It was a style that I never would have worn; teased up, long on the sides, curly with bangs, lots of hair.

She pulled down the pink pillbox hat and said, "This is perfect. No one could miss you dressed like this. Everyone will think you are such a cute *doll*."

I stared. I really thought I looked like I had hair everywhere, but Charlene said once I had the costume on, it would all blend in. The pink suit and hat, the yellow hair, the pink shoes, and a pink purse they had for me. How could I miss?

"Okay, you're done here," she said. "You must go to the director's office and find out what day you are going to be on and what time you have to report." She directed me toward the stage door entrance and told me to just wait by the guard's office. "See you soon." She waved as she rushed by me to get ready for the actors who needed her makeup skills.

What a Doll!

The guard called me into his office and gave me a phone number to use the next day to find out my show date and time. I thanked him and turned once again to stare at the backstage area. *Not today, Jane, but soon.* It was almost 7:00 p.m. when I left and it was dark. People were rushing around New York to get dinner and get ready to see a Broadway show. The corner of 45th Street and 8th Avenue is right near Times Square, and at that hour, there is always congestion. It made me feel alive, and I thought how lucky I was to be on the verge of living out one of my childhood fantasies, actually the biggest one, to be on Broadway. How could I have ever known that volunteering to help others would take me on this path? It seemed unreal.

Thursday, I called the office at 2:00 p.m. I had learned that many theater people were not working before noon, and I did not want to seem overly anxious. The voice that answered the phone was talking rapidly. "Who are you? What is this about? Oh, Broadway Cares bid to appear. Hold on."

Another voice came on immediately. "How was your day yesterday? I hope everything went well."

"Yes," I said. "I was just a little nervous."

"Not a problem. Everyone is. Even the stars of the show are nervous before the curtain comes up. You can do it. You will have plenty of help. Now I've chosen next Wednesday night. You need to be at the theater at 5:00 p.m. and report to Charlene first. She will do your hair and makeup, and then you will get your costumes. We are already writing what we are putting in the program as BCEFA gave us information on you. You will take your bow at the end of the show. Everyone knows you are coming so they will all welcome you warmly. Break a leg. Oh, any questions?" Before I could even speak—"None. Good. Well then, we will see you next week. Good-bye."

Click.

It was really going to happen; only a week away. I had a list of things to bring, and I knew the scenes I would be in. I had my costumes selected, my wig chosen, all the accoutrements. They had given me four house seat tickets, and if I wanted more friends to come, they could buy tickets at a discount. It was going to be easy. I'd been on stage before. I knew stage left, stage right, where the microphone was, and I didn't even have to sing. But it was still unnerving. People would be looking at me. But they would be looking at plenty of other people as well. Except for that one time, that cross in front of the curtain, under the moonlight with a handsome man. Wait a minute. I hadn't even met him. What if I was bigger than he was, or he didn't like me, or— I was thinking too much. Had to stop. Concentrate on my real life. Dresses to make, outfits to sew, jackets to embellish, and a store to run. Broadway had to wait.

On Broadway

4:00 p.m. Almost time to go. I had packed my bag with my shoes, underwear, stockings, hair clips, etc. My friends Annie Santiago and Avé were coming, and of course, my boyfriend Ernie. He was bringing his friend Joey. I don't know why because I didn't know him that well. He and his girlfriend were people that we went dancing with on Friday or Saturday nights. Ernie said Joey had never been to a Broadway show so this would be a treat for him. My client, Lori Kadish, also wanted to come, and she planned to include six or seven friends. That made approximately eleven people who would be looking for me in the audience. I told my friends that I would be in a costume, so be prepared to have to search for me. I even told Ernie that he might not recognize me and to look for a blonde lady. I wanted to surprise him and see if he could find me. Avé knew what costumes I would be wearing as she was going to take pictures of me getting ready for my debut. I told her not to tell anyone where I was unless they were totally oblivious. I wanted it to be a surprise.

Avé and I walked over to the theater early and checked in with the guard. He was very gracious and asked, "Are you ready?"

I smiled. "Sure."

The first place we checked in was with Sam in wardrobe. They gave me a place to keep my supplies, and I saw my outfits again. I was starting to get a little nervous, but Avé was there, and I found

119

myself posing for pictures at different stages of my preparation. Hair and makeup came first. Pin up the red hair, put on the skull cap, and adjust the wig. It was heavy but not cumbersome. The makeup girl had made my skin seem much darker than it actually was, and my eyes also appeared greenish. I rarely wore any makeup except for a bright lipstick. Without lipstick I thought I was too pale and dull looking. I never used eye makeup because my eyes appear rather sunken as I have high cheekbones and not especially large eyes. But with the makeup, they seemed to have a new life. I certainly didn't look like me in the mirror. I wondered if any of my friends would recognize me.

The pink silk suit I would change into was the most fun because it was so unlike me. Avé took some pictures of me before makeup, before wig, before costumes and after. We laughed at this new person. The playful time helped relieve the tension for me as the time to begin my preparation was coming. Laura appeared and told me to come with her to the area where I would wait. She went over my scenes, and she said for the second act, it might be easier if I stayed in the silk suit underneath a coat so I wouldn't have to make as many changes. That way when I needed to take my bow, I could just take the coat off and be ready.

"Whatever is easiest," I said.

I was actually getting anxious. Things were sinking in.

She smiled. "Everyone knows you are here, and we'll be doing everything to help you. The stage is set, and all you have to do is sit in the chair through the scene. Act like you are talking to the other people at the table and listening to the music at the nightclub. When the scene is over, walk with John, your date for the night, to the side of the stage. The two of you will wait there for the cross. Keep the pink hat on, and then after the scene for the second act, you will take it off. That way, when you are wearing the coat at the Salvation Army scenes, no one will know you still have the pink suit on. Do you want to put the pink hat on for your bow?"

"No, not at all," was my response. "Please tell me about this bow. I really don't have to do the bow. Just being here is enough."

"No, no, no. You have to take the bow. There is a little inset in the program about you, and people will want to acknowledge you. It gives the Broadway community an opportunity to tell people about Broadway Cares, and perhaps other people will want to have the same experience."

"John, please come and meet your partner for the evening," Laura called out. A tall lanky man walked over to me and took my hand. I remember him telling me how great I looked, not to be nervous, and enjoy. This was my night he said, and he was going to take me under his wing and make sure I had the best possible experience. He showed me where we would cross and told me that while we were crossing, we would just talk to each other about nothing and pretend we were on a date out for a stroll in the moonlight.

"Easy for you," I started to say when Sam tapped me on the shoulder.

"You forgot your little evening bag. Put it on the table for the first scene and wear it while you do your cross. And wear these white gloves, as well. Ladies always wore gloves then."

"Thank you, Sam. I'm sorry I forgot these."

"No worries. Break a leg, kid."

Then it was almost show time. The audience was filling. I peeked out from a side curtain with John at my side. I hadn't been formally introduced to the cast, but everyone seemed to know me.

"Thanks for being here."

"Have a great night."

"Welcome to the company."

I was feeling truly special.

Five minutes.

"Places everyone," the stage manager said.

John took me to my table. It was prominently in front of the stage on the left looking out, which is considered stage right. The curtain would be lifting soon. John took my hand across the table and whispered, "Okay?"

"Yes," I said quietly. *It's show time.*

The orchestra finished playing. The curtain rose. The magic of the theater was within me. Should I stare at the audience or look at John? The actors on stage were whispering around me and the show had begun. The scene was set at a nightclub. I had a glass in front of me. A waiter came over and whispered, "Do you want something to drink?"

I whispered back, "No, thank you," but he put a glass full of water on the table.

"It looks real when you pretend to drink," he said smiling.

John and I raised our glasses and pretended to toast. People were singing. A little dance was going on in a faux stage on the *real* stage. The audience was applauding. John grabbed my hand; time to go stage left where we'd wait for the cross.

John told me to watch from the side until he returned to cross with me. I saw so many things—tables were moved, actors racing back from left to right. Scenery coming up from under the stage. A segment with just two stars and the rest of us standing on the side watching. Some dancers were stretching while other actors stood perfectly still. It was almost as if we were in another world. No one mentioned the audience. I was starting to drift mentally.

"Are you ready, Jane?"

It was John. He took my hand and placed it through his arm. He put me on the outside of him so I could be seen and he said, "Go."

Music played. The curtain was closed behind us and I could see the audience, but I faced in toward my date, and we whispered about the moonlight as we walked from left to right. I kept my focus on him so as not to be nervous, and he made it easy for me. My legs had been shaking, but I did it.

He hugged me and said, "You were great. Gotta go. See you later."

And he was off. I stayed on that side until intermission. The first act was done. Only the second act remained. But there were many scenes, and I had to find my coat and return my purse and hat. I rushed to wardrobe and Sam said, "I was coming to you. Go on back up, and I'll meet you later to get the coat before your bow."

I kept thinking about my friends. I had tried to see them from the stage, but I was not successful. What if no one knew me? Of course Avé would. At least she could tell everyone. Since it was a great classic show, I was sure they were having a good time. But I wasn't able to focus on them and needed to be ready for the second act. I wore a heavy Salvation Army cape and had to make sure it stayed closed over my pink suit.

John came to me again and showed me where I would stand when the curtain came up. "I'm not in this scene so you just wait until everyone leaves and exit stage left."

"Okay."

In that scene, all the Salvation Army ladies had to be very disapproving because Miss Adelaide, the star, was lamenting the fact that she was falling in love with a gangster. The chorus was supposed to be angry with her, and I did my best to seem unhappy. By that time, when I was on stage, I felt as if I was part of the story. The scene ended quickly, and I went to the side and waited. I watched John dance in the next scene, and the gangsters were all over the floor, dancing on tables, singing, shouting. This was a scene that was full of life and when it was over, the audience applauded wildly. The curtain came down and John appeared again. The gangsters would be talking to some of the Salvation Army ladies. We would be looking down at them as Miss Adelaide and her gangster beau conversed. This was my last scene, and John stood staring at me with his arms at his side as if pleading with me to understand. I kept shaking my head. For that moment I forgot I was on stage. Then it was over. Sam was there to take my coat. John took me to the right side and said the next two scenes would go quickly. The final number was a roaring show-stopper with the two couples uniting and the cast singing the final song.

Then everyone would come backstage for their curtain call. As the actors took their bows, Sam stayed by my side.

"What happens now?" I asked.

"Just wait," he whispered.

All of a sudden, John was walking across the stage to get me while the male star was speaking. "And I'd like to introduce you to our special guest performer, Jane Elissa Meyers who has generously supported BCEFA to be here tonight. Let's have some applause for Jane Elissa."

John took me from the side to the center of the stage where I bowed. I finally stared into the audience. I was trying to see people but the lights were too bright. I knew I was shaking. The star was talking again, but I have no idea what he said. Then the microphone was in my hand. I think I thanked the cast and everyone who had helped me, and then there was applause. The orchestra was playing, and we were all bowing. John was hugging me and I kept thanking him. The play was done. The night was waiting and so were my friends.

Sam just stared at me as I brought my friends into the wardrobe room. They had been waiting for me by the stage door, and Laura let me take them down to my changing room. I had not put on street clothes yet because they all wanted pictures with me in my costume. So there I was, pink suit, blonde wig and my hat, all ready to hug everyone. I could not understand everything that was being said because Annie and Avé were talking at once. Lori introduced me to her friends. Who could remember their names? I was trying to explain to Ernie that I had been in four scenes because Avé told me that Ernie asked her where I was after the first act. He had totally missed me! I warned him that I was in costume, but apparently he did not know me as well as I thought he did. Spend eight years with someone, and they still can't find you on a crowded stage or even on a moonlit walk.

We were all laughing, posing, and exploring the costumes when Sam said, "You have to leave. One minute after 11:00 p.m. and it is overtime for the producers and then we get docked."

"Really," I asked?

"That's true. So give me the costume and be gone," he said as he waved his hand as if to shoo a fly.

"We are out of here," I said.

I went behind a screen, took off my pink suit, and grabbed my gear (which Ernie then took), and everyone followed me up the stairs. The night air was cool, and I realized that I did not have my coat on. Lori was saying good-bye and her friends were thanking me for letting them come. Avé had to catch a train, and Annie hadn't eaten, yet, so she was leaving also.

Ernie put my left arm through the coat he was holding, and I felt the chill of the winter air. Joey asked me if I wanted to get dinner with him and Ernie, but I said no because I was exhausted. I turned to wave to everyone else and hugged Miss Adelaide as she came out of the stage door before I put my arm through Ernie's to walk home. They questioned me about backstage and my experience, and I began to cry. I was not sad, but I was relieved and that relief manifested itself in tears. Joey walked to the side as we stopped and Ernie held me.

I kept saying, "I'm fine."

But Ernie said, "Let it out. You need this release. You had a big night and now it is over."

How right he was. *It was over.* I would probably never do it again, and I felt so happy and sad at the same time. I just wanted to go home and be alone. I said good-bye to Joey and gave Ernie a long hug and a lingering kiss and he said, "I'll see you tomorrow."

That was all I remember before closing my eyes and going to bed. I had lived my earliest dream....

Michael J. Fox

*I*n the mid 90s, Michael J. Fox was taping a comedy series called *Spin City* at Chelsea Piers. Through a friend, I was introduced to a man named Peter Smith, who had survived a rare form of leukemia. He came to the shop and told me his story, and what he had gone through in terms of chemotherapy and radiation. It was a long struggle for him, and I asked him to tell his story at one of our events. I wanted people to see the face of leukemia and learn how it could strike anyone at any time. There stood a young man who was struck in his teens and worked through his fear and anxiety to become a healthy adult. He was even going to be married.

I invited Peter to a sports-oriented event that was held in partnership with Madison Square Garden. It was called the "Meet the Announcer's Luncheon." The sports broadcasters became waiters and served the patrons at the Garden, and the money raised from the tickets purchased was given to the Leukemia Society. Ernie, Peter, and I attended these lunches, and we were waited on by superstar Walt Frasier of the New York Knicks, who actually offered to come to one of my events, announcers Marv and Steve Albert, and John Andrease, who became very involved with the Leukemia Society but has since passed on.

The Garden paid for students in the New York City schools to attend, and I was able to bid on sports memorabilia. Of course I could not resist that, so I now own footballs signed by some of the New York Jets and a baseball signed by Yogi Berra. One of the other packages I won was the opportunity to go to a Mets game and watch from the press box and meet and hear the announcers do the play-by-play. *That* was a *super* treat but the best part of that luncheon was watching the announcers run around and try to be waiters. There was a lot of spillage and quick movements around the tables, but it was a refreshing way to spend two hours, and Peter was happy to meet Walt Frasier.

Another surprise I had planned for Peter was a special visit to the set of the television show *Spin City*. One of the producers had come into the shop at the Marriott and purchased some Jane Elissa hats. She saw our "wall" and asked if I ever needed any nighttime celebrities for my event. I said I would love it but hadn't been able to reach anyone. She gave me her card and said to give her a call. She would see what she could arrange. I also told her how much Peter Smith loved the show and about his struggle to beat leukemia. Two days later, she called me and told me that we could come to a taping of *Spin City* and meet Michael J. Fox afterward. We would have to get there by 4:00 p.m., wait in line, and sit in the audience through a dry run before they taped. The show was shot at Chelsea Piers, and it would not finish until around 11:00 p.m. But Peter was fine with that. The producer allowed me to take a couple others so I invited Ernie and my friend Annie Albarian to go along. I anticipated meeting Michael and asking for something signed for our auction, or better yet, if he would like to make an appearance at our benefit. That would have been something special.

The Chelsea Piers Theater was not warm. They were shooting in the middle of winter on the water, and it was chilly. I had worn a sweater under a warm coat and heavy winter boots. I kept my coat on throughout the performance, and by the end, I had put on my gloves. It was all worth it as we were entertained by the warm-up person and watched the interaction of putting on a live show. There were signs that said applause, others that said laughter, and even quiet ones. I never knew that all of the laughter was planned. We did not need to be instructed to laugh because the show was naturally funny, and we felt like we were actually a part of the process. It was great fun.

I had been told to meet a producer, Maria, after the show on the left side of the stage. We waited until the audience had cleared out and then looked for her. A production assistant brought her out to us about ten minutes later, and she told us to wait because Michael was very tired and needed a little time to rest.

"Don't worry. We'll wait," I said. "We won't take much of his time."

Maria nodded and left us standing by the side of the audience entrance. About twenty minutes later, she came out with Michael. He had a big smile and stood opposite us. I was a little intimidated because I thought he was a very special talent, and I did not want to seem too pushy.

"Thanks for coming," he said. "Did you enjoy the show?"

Of course we all said yes at once, and we proceeded to tell him what parts made us laugh the most. He smiled and explained how many times they had gone over the dialogue prior to the "run through" to make it just right. I introduced him specifically to Peter, and they shook hands quietly. I did notice he kept his hands in his pockets and shifted his feet, but I had no idea what was developing with his health.

Maria again thanked us for coming, and I expressed my appreciation for Michael taking the time to meet with us. It was almost midnight, and I was sure he was exhausted, but he agreed to pose for a picture with us all, and then Maria said he had to leave. Before he went back to his dressing room, he turned back to me and said, "If you ever need anything, just let Maria know. I think it's great the work you are doing."

I smiled and then he was gone. I had always thought I would call her again for tickets to the show as an auction package, but soon after, it was announced he was fighting Parkinson's. What a gentleman he had been—he took the time to see us and make us feel welcome. His kindness was to remain in my mind for a long time, and I wrote them a personal thank you note. God bless Michael J. Fox.

Peter Smith, Jane Elissa, Michael J. Fox,
Ernie Gonzalez & Dr. Annie Albarian

Laurie Beechman

*A*s entertaining as it had been to meet Michael J. Fox, getting to know Laurie Beechman was equally fulfilling. Prior to the eighth year of my benefit, I had attended a performance of the Broadway show *CATS*. I went with a dear friend named John who also loved the theater. The actress playing the role of Grizabella was named Laurie Beechman. She had the most amazing voice, as it always had a hearty sound, and it was throaty but lush. To this day, I have never heard another voice like hers.

I became a fan and purchased her CDs. Whenever she appeared at clubs in New York, I would try to get tickets. I had never met her, but always wanted to tell her how much I appreciated her voice. I could never have planned what was to come.

My shop was doing well, and Avé enjoyed being the manager and working in the back room. We spent a lot of time hunting down new items to keep the store "exciting and fresh." Every Friday, we had to stock the jewelry cases, because on the weekends, the tourists and matinee crowd would come, and we needed to keep them happy. I spent much of the week in my apartment creating designs to sell. I liked working by myself because I accomplished more alone. I did, however, have other obligations, including meeting with the Leukemia Society and planning my events. I also filled in at the shop when needed and stopped in at least three to four times a week.

We were lucky to have interns from the New York City school system to train because they helped enormously. I went back to the system to teach some master classes, and I felt that we were contributing to the students' artistic growth with experience in the shop.

I had purchased tickets for Ernie and I to attend Laurie Beechman's performance at a Rainbow and Stars Cabaret. The Saturday before I was to see Laurie, I had to cover a shift for one of my workers. Usually before the matinees, between 1:00 p.m. and 2:00 p.m., there was a mad rush of people. Whether they bought or not was something else. Nevertheless they were in the store, looking for mostly inexpensive, unusual items and they needed attention. On one particular day, there were a lot of lookers. I stayed at the cash register while Janelle (our trainee) helped the clients. An older lady came in with her husband and started looking at some of our hand-painted, embellished jackets. She was a quiet, elegant woman who seemed very impressed with my handmade garments. Her husband waited for her on the sofa we had in the back of the shop. I decided to help her because she seemed genuinely interested in purchasing some jackets and shawls. We talked and she chose two of my more expensive embroidered pieces.

When I brought them to the register for her to pay, she told me the items were for her daughter who was an actress. I said, "Oh, I hope she likes them."

She said she was sure she would and took some of my cards because she knew her friends might like my work as well. I sat down and took her credit card. I began asking questions about her daughter. She told me she had been on Broadway and was working on another album. As I totaled up her receipt and put the card in, I noticed the name—the middle name on the card was Beechman. I was stunned. I stared at her and quietly asked, "Is your daughter Laurie Beechman?"

She smiled and said yes.

I almost fell off my chair. "I can't believe it," I stammered. "I am a huge fan. I have followed her in *CATS*, and I am going to see her next weekend at Rainbow and Stars."

Dolly looked at me and we exchanged Laurie Beechman stories. But even better than that, she promised to tell Laurie I was coming to see her and ask if she would grant me a backstage visit. I was floating on air. I was actually going to meet one of my favorite Broadway performers, and Dolly said that once Laurie opened her presents, she would be excited to know me. It started to sink in that my art to wear was being recognized. I was not sure what expectation this would create and a sense of fear came upon me. I don't know why, but it was there.

∞

Ernie and I were not familiar with the cabaret, Rainbow and Stars. We went to Rockefeller Center early, but we could not find the entrance. The Rockefeller Center building is very tall and considering my aversion to elevators, I was very wary of taking one "to the top of the rock," as they say. I just closed my eyes and followed Ernie into the elevator and held my breath. My ears popped as we arrived, and I cautiously peered out to a beautifully decorated entrance with pink flowers and green trees and then I saw the windows. It seemed like the entire side of the building was overlooking Manhattan. The lights shone. I could even see people walking for a brief time and I stood there. A little too high for me— but a twilight universe nonetheless.

I had spoken to Laurie's mom a few days before, and she told me Laurie would love for us to visit. She warned me that after a performance, she might be a little bit tired, but she really wanted to meet me. I was wearing a very simple dress with one of my Victorian inspired black velvet shawls. Ernie had on a suit and a tie as that was the dress code at this supper club. We were seated at a table away from the stage but with a center view, and the people near us all seemed to be fans from the theater. I overheard a couple talking about having seen her in *Joseph and the Amazing Technicolor Dream Coat*, and other plays that I did not know, but

133

I could not wait to hear her sing again.

I don't remember what the food tasted like, but I do remember the applause that greeted Laurie when she was introduced. She was a lot smaller than I imagined, with short dark hair and huge brown eyes. She was wearing a black dress with a cream jacket and some crystal earrings. She sparkled. Then there was *the voice* — one hour of endless musical pleasure, every note crisp, tones that were mellow but strong and then the signature "Memory" from *CATS*, which I cried through. Everyone was on their feet when she came out for her encore, and I felt like I had heard the best singing ever. A reminder again of why I was not a performer.

When the applause finally ended and Laurie made her exit, I went to the maître de and told him that we were there to see her. He looked at me quickly, asked my name, and directed me to a small hallway in front of a locked door. That was her dressing room. He told me to wait until someone opened the door and then I could enter. Ernie stayed in the background because we were not sure if she wanted to see anyone other than me. Some singers need time to unwind after a performance and don't really want anyone around. Others are on a high and enjoy the attention and adoration of their fans. Since I did not know Laurie, I was not sure which category she fell into, so Ernie and I agreed I would proceed first.

After waiting about ten minutes, the door opened and someone told me to come in. Laurie was sitting by the mirror, and she turned and smiled at me. "So you're Jane Elissa. I love my shawl and jacket. You are so talented."

She extended her hand. I took it and said, "No, you are the talented one."

We both laughed. She told me her mother had raved about my shop, and she wanted to come by in the near future to see what other items I might have. From then on, we both babbled about theater, acting, singing, and who knows what else. Finally, she seemed a little tired and she walked me to the door. She saw Ernie standing in the hallway and asked if he was with me. I said yes and introduced her. "Lucky you," she said. "You have a handsome friend."

I glanced at Ernie and saw him light up and thanked her. We exchanged phone numbers and promised to get together once her gig at Rainbow and Stars was done. I thanked her and told her again what a great time I had and then floated to the elevator. How many floors up were we? I didn't care. It had been an absolutely wonderful evening.

☃

Hearing and seeing Laurie Beechman had brought back some pleasant as well as painful memories for me. I had always loved the theater, and as a young girl, I participated in school plays and sang in the choir, which I enjoyed. Because music teachers liked my voice, I was often chosen to sing solos. This did not appeal to me. I was not a natural performer, and although I liked singing in the chorus, I did *not* enjoy being the star. I was too afraid to say no to the teachers so I accepted the solos. But before I had to sing, I would be terrified and often thought I would lose my voice. And, of course, one time I did. I opened my mouth and only a hoarse rasp came out. Again—I tried—nothing but the rasp. Finally, my voice came and I sang the song, but the fear remained, and I never sang solo again.

To this day, I still remember the shame I felt with my father in the audience. Although a kind and endearing man, my father was a bit of a perfectionist when it came to show biz. He had been a comedian in the Borscht Belt before he gave it up to become an attorney. He *loved* to perform and felt totally comfortable with the spotlight. He was a terrific actor and that ability made him a terrific trial attorney. He could really focus on a jury and convince them of what he was saying. His clients loved him, but he saw my mistake that night as a terrible error, and we said absolutely nothing on the ride home. Not a pleasant memory.

I also studied on Saturday at the American Academy of Dramatic Arts (AADA). I was accepted after doing a stage reading, and I thought I would find out if I had any potential in show business. Even though I did not want to be the star, I did enjoy performing on stage *with other people*. When I got up there, it became a real world, and I would forget there was even an audience. Still, it took a lot for me to get on stage. Being a student at the American Academy of Dramatic Arts actually helped me make the decision that I did not want to be in show business. Although I had a lyrical soprano voice, significant dance talent, and was an adequate enough actress, I did *not* have the desire to compete for parts or the ability to let my emotions go and act my heart out in front of people. I was awed by the talent at that school. The students were not just gifted, they were truly motivated. They *wanted* the spotlight and regardless of talent, they would work harder and compete stronger than I ever would. They took rejection as it came and plowed into the next opportunity. That was not for me. I had to find something else.

The reason I tell you this is so that you can understand when I point out the irony of my having a shop in the middle of Times Square and staging fashion shows while working with actors, people whose needs I definitely understood. It was as if the fates had conspired to bring me back to the theatrical world I had left a long time before. No amount of planning could have predicted this turn of events. I did not have an artist's store on the beach. I had my name in gold engraving on a shop, on the eighth floor lobby of the largest hotel on Broadway, in the middle of the New York theater district. It wasn't in the original plan and yet there I was.

೫

Because of my growing friendship with Laurie and the admiration I had for her and other Broadway stars, I decided to add an award to the benefit. I called it "The Shining Star Award" and I gave it to a Broadway celebrity who had either developed, over time, an amazing Broadway resume or who had performed a "star turn," meaning they'd had an exceptional year on stage.

Not only did it recognize their talent, but it also recognized their charitable commitments. The first person I wanted to honor was Laurie Beechman. She had shone on Broadway for many years, and I was certain she deserved it. I also knew a little secret that she had shared with my mother in my shop. She had ovarian cancer and she had been fighting it for a long time. She confided this to my mother when they were having a conversation on the sofa in the shop. She told Mom because she wanted my mother to know she empathized with her battle with leukemia. I was not there for that conversation, but my mother told me she felt very close to Laurie at the moment.

I contacted Laurie and told her about the "shining star" award. At first she was hesitant as she wasn't sure how she would feel. She talked it over with her manager and her husband, and told me everyone agreed it would be a lovely honor. I hugged her and we sat down to talk briefly about her illness. She was one of the most courageous people I had ever met. She was on medication, wearing wigs, had a shunt in her chest, and she was singing her heart out. She also was working on a new CD called *No One is Alone*, and this event would give her an opportunity to introduce it. Whatever she needed, I told her I would do.

I called the Leukemia Society and asked to speak with Kerri Dubler, my coordinator at the time. She asked me to come to the office to discuss what I had in mind. We made an appointment for the following week, and I started to think about the scope of what I might be undertaking.

No One Is Alone

I sat down with Laurie at the Edison Hotel restaurant on 47th Street and Broadway. She had chosen the place because it was quiet and not too crowded. Laurie thanked me for wanting to honor her, and we talked about her battle with ovarian cancer. She told me these years were some of the best ones she had in her life. She had gotten married in spite of the disease, was booked to perform at Rainbow and Stars Cabaret with Sam Harris, and would be doing *Les Miz* in Philadelphia (her hometown) at the Walnut Street Theater.

She was upbeat but very serious about making the fundraiser profitable and (after I confessed that we weren't always overly organized) a little more professional than it had been. She gave me the names of people she thought could help me—Jim Wilhelm, Overland, Andrew Lloyd Weber's the Really Useful Company, and Andy Harmon. Laurie told me to speak to them about the show as they would have ideas. She also gave me lists of people to contact for prizes, attendance, and donations. It was a girl-talk afternoon as well as an event-planning session. I was thrilled to see her laughing with me. She also reminded me she was releasing her CD, *No One is Alone*, and I thought that would be a perfect theme for the night.

I followed up immediately with the names she had given me. Jean Rooney was able to get her company to sponsor us again, and the same printers were willing to make the invitations and print the programs. Walt Willey agreed to be the host, and Clint Holmes returned as our musical host. All these professional people were with me again, and I had confidence that we could put the show together the way Laurie would want it.

Walt Willey & Jane

I called Andy Harmon and introduced myself as the "benefit for Laurie lady." His secretary put him on the phone immediately and from that first conversation, I felt an easiness talking to him. He *loved* Laurie's voice and said he would do anything he could to help. Although he had never met me, he invited me to go with him and his wife to see Laurie and Sam Harris perform at Rainbow and Stars. I agreed immediately because I wanted his advice on whatever needed to be done, and if I could be with him for a few hours in a casual setting, I thought I would learn a lot. I had no idea what he or his wife was like, but he seemed so pleasant on the phone that I just accepted his offer.

Andy and his wife became a part of "the Jane Elissa universe." They were so supportive of the effort I was putting together that I followed almost all of his suggestions. He told me that after he first heard Laurie perform, he hired her to do corporate concerts for Seagram's all over the country. He was *that* enamored with her voice. Overland Entertainment was the producer of those concerts, and Andy told me to talk to them about getting Laurie and her people what they needed for the event. I had no idea what needs they might have, but I agreed.

A few days later, I met with a production team, Jim Wilhelm, her agent, and a stage manager. We were finally going to have a line producer who would put the show together in a timeline and plan out every detail. This forced me to sit down and approximate how many minutes it would take the models for each of their segments. I also worked with Clint on timing his songs, Neil with the length of his piano performance, and Walt with how long it would take to give awards, welcome everyone, conduct live auctions, etc. This was all a huge change! I would learn an invaluable tool for the future—how to write a minute-by-minute show plan.

We planned a VIP reception which allowed the higher ticket purchasers to have a private meeting with the stars at 6:00 p.m. After that, everyone would have a seated dinner, and then the show would start at 8:00 p.m. The committee members found volunteers to check everyone in and escort people to their seats. Because I was always running around at the events, the evening was a blur. I had to remain backstage to coordinate the models and cue everyone for the show. The stage manager was there also, but his main concerns were making sure the singers were prepared, the monitors were ready, and the sound system worked. Neil Berg, who had joined me for prior shows, would play the piano during the fashion show. Everyone knew their jobs. This show had to run smoothly. I had Andrew Lloyd Weber's people there, and the Broadway talent was top notch. I do not know how I was able to stand up under the weight of wanting everything to be right. Having Jean Rooney out front really helped.

Sean McDermott, who would later become a huge supporter of our events, opened the Broadway segment with "Starlight Express." I put him in a shiny silver suit because the "starlights" would reflect off the silver. He told the story of working with Laurie and that the show was done on roller skates. One evening as he was singing, he skated right into the first row of the audience. The shocked women there helped him up, and he kept right on singing. His rendition of "Starlight Express" that night was flawless.

Everyone who performed, including Loni Ackerman, Catherine Hickland, Karen Mason, and Ron Raines, was wonderful. There was, however, one person who awed us all. I snuck out to hear him sing and that was Davis Gaines. He was appearing in *Phantom of the Opera* as the phantom, and he sang "Music of the Night." The audience, which consisted of some people who were still eating, was not always as quiet as I would have liked. When Davis sang, I could not hear another sound. People just stopped whatever they were doing and listened, including me. I was tingling and screaming while applauding when he finished. Everyone was on their feet.

The night finished with Sam Harris, the presentation of the Shining Star Award, and Laurie performing "No One is Alone." By then I was in the audience with some of the backstage help and committee members, and I listened to Laurie's acceptance speech. She spoke movingly about her career and her personal battles, and she thanked us for recognizing her. I cried when she sang, and I finally experienced a sense of accomplishment and gratitude to God for giving me the courage to do these events. It was a moment of self-acknowledgement that I was beginning to allow myself, and I felt very fulfilled.

Andy/Seagram's Corp.

After our event honoring Laurie Beechman, I stayed in touch with Andy Harmon and his wife. We occasionally had dinner and talked a lot about our mutual admiration of Laurie. They also became fans of my work and made some purchases in my shop. For Christmas, I gave Andy's wife a beautiful floral tapestry bag that we had created. I do not remember what I gave him, but I know that bag launched me into a new project.

About a month later, I received a phone call from Andy's office at Seagram's. Although I knew he worked there, I had never known what his official capacity was. His secretary asked if I would come by for a meeting that day as Andy wanted to discuss a premium gift with me. I had no idea what that was, but I agreed. She asked me if I had samples of my tapestry bags, and if I did, to bring them.

The Seagram's offices were located in the Seagram's Building. It was a tall, corporate structure, and Andy's office was large and filled with "stuff," as I called it. Bottles, bags, hats, shirts, key chains—anything you could think of that people sell. I thought to myself—

Why does he have all this stuff? But I said nothing.

As usual, he was as charming and pleasant as ever but he got right to the point. "I love your bags," he said. "Show me what you have."

I took out three tapestry bags in different shapes.

"Can you make me a bag with the Seagram's logos that I can give next Christmas to all my best clients? I want it to be a shape for men or women in a unisex tapestry fabric." He then pulled out a bag he had given out at a golf tournament and asked me if I could use that design shape for our creation.

"Of course," I said. "Whatever you need, but I'll need all your logos for your products so I can incorporate them in my design."

He rang someone on the intercom, and in two minutes, I had pictures of all the wonderful Seagram's products. Since I am not a person who drinks a lot, I was very unfamiliar with these names. But they would become my "bosom buddies" over time.

I had no idea how I was going to fulfill Andy's request because I had never actually designed a tapestry pattern for a textile company to produce. I usually bought already printed tapestries (often with New York City themes) and then made them into bags, jackets, etc. This "project" would be a totally new challenge, and I was not even sure how to go about doing it. But I did not want to disappoint Andy, and I would never admit to myself that any artistic endeavor was impossible. I had to find a way.

At the time, I was buying tapestry fabric from a company in Canada. They had representatives in North Carolina who I dealt with. I called their office and presented my dilemma. They told me if I created a design they could produce it, but there was a minimum yardage amount, a setup expense, a design fee, and shipping costs. They would need money in advance and a written purchase order from Seagram. I was to formulate my design, overnight it to them, and work out all the colors with their design team. This was going to be a large undertaking.

I told Andy what I needed to do, and he said he would have a check ready immediately when he approved my design. After many reworkings, we were ready. I had an invoice from the tapestry company, and Andy wrote out a purchase order and issued the check. Then he handed me a check as a project manager designer. I had not submitted a bill yet, but he wanted to give me a deposit.

"Let me know how much you think the bags will be, and I'll give you a deposit for them as well. Make sure you are covering your time and expenses," he said.

I had not even thought about the scope of this project or how much it would cost. I did not even know how many bags were needed, but I knew there would be more than enough yardage for anything else he might want. I was on my way.

The project would take a long time, and I learned part of Andy's job was to buy premium gifts. This was a whole industry I knew nothing about, but I did discover that people made a lot of money servicing companies and producing specialty items for them. Since I knew how much many of these products cost, I was shocked at some of the prices people were charging Andy. I told him if he ever needed price quotes on items to call me as I would at least be able to tell him what I thought a fair price to pay would be.

I did create another product for him—a Crown Royal crystal purse, which no one he was working with seemed to be able to do at a reasonable price. I called upon my friend Eddie from Rachel & Co. who made crystal bags overseas. Between us, he and I worked out a price structure that saved Andy money, but still enabled us to earn a respectful profit. We used beautiful Italian crystals and made the bag look exactly like the Crown Royal bottle. I knew his clients would love it.

I think back on that chance meeting with Andy, and I remember that this huge project all came about because of our mutual admiration of Laurie Beechman. And that goes back to the Leukemia Benefit and the volunteering to help I had done. That phone call to the Leukemia Society all those years ago had proven to be the best ten-cent phone call I had ever made.

Annie Santiago on Broadway

Because my friend Annie Santiago had been so generous in loaning me part of the start-up capital for my shop, I wanted to do something special for her. Having the Seagram's project helped me pay Annie back quickly, but I needed to show my appreciation by giving her something special. I found out after I "lived my dream" that she had always wanted to be an actress. I had never known that and once she told me, I knew how I was going to surprise her. I would bid on the opportunity for her to be in a Broadway show the same way I had been. This was something she would never give herself, and it would be a once in a lifetime experience.

I went again to the Broadway Cares flea market. Pat came with me, and I told her we had to bid on a walk-on for my friend. Luckily it was overcast and drizzling that day which deterred people from coming outside to bid in Shubert Alley. There were a few shows available that day, but as time went on, they were taken by very zealous bidders. I did not have ten thousand dollars to spend, and I was becoming disheartened as it was getting near the end of the auction. Pat pointed out that there was one more show—*Grease*—and she noticed that the crowd was thinning. The rain was starting to really come down, but I was not going to leave without getting a walk-on. I waited patiently and finally the

147

auctioneer said, "Our last appearance on Broadway is for the show *Grease*. Let's open the bidding at five hundred dollars."

I watched—anyone's hand up—of course, two people, three people—fifteen hundred dollars—two thousand—quiet.

"Anyone else?" she asked.

"Twenty-five hundred," I said.

Everyone looked. It was my first bid.

Everyone was quiet—again—

"Any other bids?"

No, let's get on with it, I thought.

"Twenty-six hundred"—from out of nowhere.

"Twenty-seven-fifty," I said.

Silence again.

"Anyone else?" the auctioneer asked.

Not a sound—waiting for what was an eternally long minute....

"*Sold* for twenty-seven hundred and fifty dollars to the lady with the pink hat."

Hooray, I thought, I really got it. What a great surprise this will be. I could not wait to tell Annie. The prize was an extra special walk-on because it included a black leather jacket with pink rhinestones spelling out Grease on the back. It also came with house seats and the opportunity to participate in rehearsals on stage at the theater. Of course, I told Annie I had to come to the rehearsal. I wanted to share in the experience. Perhaps that was selfish of me, but I enjoyed watching how shows came together, and I was indulging my love for theater as well.

Annie appeared in more scenes than I had. She even got to be in a "hula hoop" background number. It was so much fun for me to watch her on the stage. Avé, Ernie, Annie's good friend Marilyn, her mother and sister, and I went. We just hooted and applauded every time she came out.

Jon Secada was Danny Zuko, the lead and his voice really captured the feeling of that era. Of course, we went backstage afterward, and Ernie bonded with Jon. They were both Cuban, and they spoke in Spanish in Jon's dressing room for a long time. It was a very special moment for Ernie to be able to talk about the country he had left behind. I busied myself talking to some of the other actors and exploring backstage. It was almost as magical a night as my debut because someone else's dream had been fulfilled, and I was instrumental in helping to make it happen. So much joy and fun that night....

British Airways

$\mathcal{A}$ woman named Karen Haas had attended the evening honoring Laurie Beecham. She loved Broadway and asked me if I would put on a cabaret performance for her company British Airways. Karen offered to sponsor the event and have her people help with everything but the show. I did not need to have a fashion show—just have daytime celebrities as guest hosts or presenters of talent. It seemed like another challenge, but one I should not refuse. More money as well as awareness could be raised for the charity, so what was holding me back?

...With each step forward comes more responsibility—find a new venue, work with new people, produce a different show—and at the same time run a retail and wholesale business in a very busy hotel. Fill more space in my life so I do not have to look at my life. Was that what I really wanted?

If I was going to do another fundraiser that year, I needed a partner. I found a comrade in Loraine Jacobs. She offered to work with me on the British Airways cabarets. What a blessing that was. I now had someone whose judgment I respected and who could help me make decisions. All the money raised would go to the LLS, but Loraine showed me how I could control how it was dispersed. She had created a Jim Jacobs Research Fund in honor of her husband. She suggested I do the same. Then I could sponsor a researcher within the society and know what specific work was being done. I could also track the money that went in under my name and get reports from the national office. I established the JE/CM Endowment Fund at the LLS. All the proceeds would be split between Loraine's fund and mine, and that was an equitable distribution.

Working with Karen and Loraine was like a dream. They were accommodating, knowledgeable, and forthright. None of us was afraid to speak our minds. That made planning easier because everyone's views were considered. Karen took care of the printing of the invitations, the program, and the journal. She also provided volunteers to help at the event. For the first time in organizing the fundraisers, I did not feel the weight of everything on my shoulders. If there were problems, we shared them and that was a great relief. I had not realized before what stress those responsibilities had put on me.

The actual first British Airways event was held at the Supper Club in the New York theater district. It was in the spring of 1997, and the last event before the hiccups in my life. Ernie came with a friend, and although I took a moment to say hello, I had no time to spend with them. It often struck me as bittersweet when he came to my events as I was pleased he attended but sad that I could not enjoy the experience with him. I would have loved to see the evening through his eyes. The committee had gotten great prizes, I now knew how to develop a show schedule, and I had great talent on tap. The venue was an old theater converted into a dinner-dance club. It had upstairs seating looking onto the dance floor, as well as, downstairs seating on the perimeter of the space. We used the section in front of the stage to set up tables for a buffet dinner. There was a bar in the back of the room. The ticket price included the dinner, show, and two-hour open bar. After that, it was a cash bar. Sometimes I was concerned about people drinking and talking during the entertainment, but once the performers began, everyone was quiet.

For that particular performance, I let everyone choose their songs. I made suggestions, but the singers knew what they did best. One star, who I was now friends with and scheduled to be featured, was Sean McDermott. He was a bona fide Broadway "biggie." He had opened as the young lead in *Miss Saigon*, played opposite Mandy Patinkin in *Falsettos*, and would go on to star as Danny Zuko in the Broadway revival of *Grease*. He also had starred as Hart Jessup on the CBS soap opera *Guiding Light*. Not only was he tall, blue-eyed, handsome and sexy, but he could sing anything from rock 'n' roll, to Broadway, to Country Western. My most loyal and hardworking committee member Annie Albarian had become his close friend, and I loved working with them both. To this day, he is still committed to our cause. Neil Berg would play the piano again, and the wonderful cast from the Broadway show *Smokey Joe's Café,* including Fred Owens and Bobby Daye, would sing those great rock 'n' roll songs.

A new dimension that was added at that point was the cast of the spoof *Forbidden Broadway*. They were a professional troupe of singers who performed songs from the current and past Broadway seasons and poked fun at the shows. The satire had people laughing throughout. They brought exaggerated costumes and picked just the right quirks in the shows. From *Les Miz,* there's the song "Bring Him Home" sung by Jean Valjean, which is in a very high key. Their writer had Jean Valjean singing "Bring It Down." This song's "too high," this show's too long, etc. It was very, very wittily written and hysterical to watch, and they brought a lightness to the event that the audience responded well to. They returned for all the British Airways cabarets.

At the end of the night, the people British Airways had invited and all the other guests gave the performers a standing ovation. Loraine, Karen, and I were feted with flowers and congratulatory hugs. It was one of the most enjoyable events I had worked on. Karen wanted to start planning the next one immediately. Loraine and I just sighed thinking with success comes *more* responsibility. Here we go again....

Sports—Andy Robustelli

There were times when I worked with celebrities where I was still a fan—anxious, nervous upon meeting them, weak kneed, and with a few little crushes. One such person in my life was a sports icon—Andy Robustelli, who played for the New York Giants. I had a booth at a wholesale accessories show at the Javits Center to sell my products to stores, and I also had a sign there about my LLS charity work. The last two people to come by that day had a shop named Resortique in Connecticut. They were lovely women who thought our hats and jackets, camisoles, etc. would sell well as a resort line. At that time, we were hand making everything we did and things were "pricey" as it's termed in the industry. That meant that even though it was all handmade (which used to be a plus), it would have to be sold in stores that had clientele who would appreciate that and have the money to pay for it. These particular women told me they had the clientele and would like me to meet their boss who also ran a travel agency and might be able to donate some travel packages for my benefits.

I did not have time to ask about their boss because the lights were flickering at the Javits Center and that meant I had to close up my booth for the day. We exchanged cards and Pat, one of the women, told me she would call me in a few days to arrange to come to the shop. After the show, I looked at her card which also listed Robustelli Travel Services. For some reason, I did not connect Andy Robustelli with Robustelli Travel Services. When Pat called and made an appointment to come to the store, she did not mention her boss's name. We planned to meet the following week. I prepared the LLS portfolio with some of my previous events as well as an array of wholesale items they could buy for their shop. I did not get nervous because I did not know who was coming.

That day was very busy in the shop. It was a Wednesday afternoon "matinee" day and they were coming right after lunch. Avé and I were frazzled by the time they arrived, and I had no time to fix my hair or make sure my clothing was neat. In they walked— a tall, distinguished, graying man with a football player's build in a dark gray suit.... Still, I did not know him.

Avé and I shook everyone's hand and then Pat said, "And this is Andy Robustelli, our boss...."

She continued talking but I was in a fog. Thank goodness Avé was there because I was instantly a blushing fan. I could not speak. He was so handsome and refined. He walked around looking at all the women's clothing, and along with Pat and Lisa, choosing items for their shop. Avé wrote his order, and he pulled out his Resortique check to pay for what he was taking.

Finally I said, "I am a huge football fan of the New York Giants. It is such an honor to meet you...."

He smiled. "Well, it's an honor to meet you, and whatever we can do for your fundraisers, we will be happy to help."

"Thank you—"

That's all I remember of that day. I had followed Andy Robustelli and the New York Giants since I was a child. I would later learn that not only was he a Hall of Fame football player, he was also a smart and savvy businessman who'd built a conglomerate of different businesses. He was nothing like the stereotype of a dumb jock. Not only was he very handsome, but he was so kind and caring about other people, and his generosity to all my fundraisers was greatly appreciated. He adored his wife, children, and grandchildren, and had a great friendship with Pat. She has since become a friend of mine. She laughs when she tells the story of when I went to see the shop in Stamford, Connecticut. They took me to lunch, and I could not stop staring at Andy. He even drove me back to the train station that day, and I was so nervous that I barely spoke. I had such a crush on him. I own a signed copy of his book (many of which we auctioned off at the benefits) and some posters he gave me. I will always treasure these.

The Tenth Anniversary—The Beginning of the End

*I*t was going to be our biggest year yet. I had been working on these fundraisers for almost ten years, and I had a wonderful new group of friends and committee members. Being on the board at the Leukemia Society created connections with many influential people who helped with the growth of my events. I had created a specific endowment fund with the LLS, which enabled me to pick the researcher I wanted to sponsor. The opportunity allowed me to meet personally with the researchers and learn more about the work they were conducting. I could then report to my committee where the money we raised went and what area of blood cancer research we were sponsoring. When anyone from the committee spoke at our events, they would have first-hand knowledge of our accomplishments.

This was to be our anniversary year, and everyone was anxious to make it the best year ever. Since I had created the Shining Star Award for a Broadway performer, we wanted to choose someone extra special. Years before one of my clients, Margaret, had introduced me to her high school friend, Robert Cuccioli, who was then starring as Javert in *Les Miz* on Broadway. She said he was a very nice person, and she thought he would be willing to participate in our show to help the Leukemia Society.

Avé and I thought that would be great because we were trying to get to the Broadway community, and there would be a bona fide star to help us. What we weren't prepared for was how tall, dark and handsome he was, and equally as nice. He came to my shop to meet Avé and me, and Avé almost fell over. She got so quiet that I knew she was in awe of him. Whatever costume we needed him to wear, he said he would. He brought a few of his eight by ten photos to use if I needed it for the publicity, and after he left, Avé grabbed them and begged me to give her one. Of course, I did.

I became friends with Robert, who was starring in *Jekyll and Hyde* as the lead. I watched his transformation from Javert **Jane & Robert Cuccioli** to Jekyll. It was a long road as the musical changed often from the original concept to what eventually would come to Broadway. Both Bob and the leading lady, Linda Eder, did not change, but the rest of the cast varied. Finally, when it was set, we spoke on the phone, and he said he was not sure if he should do the matinees for the show as it was a very taxing role. Actor, Robert Evan (who would also later become one of my friends) would do the matinee and in the end that was for the best. It gave Bob a little time to recover from the strain of playing both Dr. Jekyll and Mr. Hyde.

His performance was recognized by the theater community as brilliant. He was enjoying the success of that show. There were tons of fans calling themselves "Jekkies" who would go to the show over and over again. I must confess I became one of those who could not see it enough. Initially I went to see Bob and be supportive of him, but once I saw the show, I wanted all my friends to go. We even told people who came into our shop to see it because it was very entertaining. It took your emotions on a roller coaster. And I loved the period costumes from the Victorian era. What a great theatrical night it was and a true star turn for him. Now that he was a big success, I wanted him to be our shining star. He deserved it. We would build our event around the theme of "Romance and Change."

We had our Charlotte Meyers Volunteer Recognition Award winners from the daytime world, and our committee wanted to be sure that we started early to plan the format of the event. I was very preoccupied that year because my dad was ill and suffering from congestive heart failure. I also knew that Laurie's condition was getting worse and that my lease for the shop would be up at the end of 1997. Ernie and I had decided that we were ready to move to Florida. I was thinking that I was finally going to have that beach house and little art store near the shore. I had a great financial contract from Seagram, and things looked very rosy. The benefit planning had been going well. My event chair was diligently putting together programs. The invitations had gone out. Robert Cuccioli was very popular and people were recognizing him. And then it happened....

Because everything was in place, I had time to concentrate on my order for Seagram. The fabric had come in from Canada and Josephine Originals was ready to make the bags. Eddie was producing the Crown Royal bags and we were on schedule. It was Labor Day weekend about a month and a half before the benefit. Ernie was spending the weekend, and we were going to be lazy and just enjoy New York City.

I also had some obligations that weekend, and Ernie agreed to help me with them. My friend Lauri Landry, who was going to be appearing in the *Scarlett Pimpernel* was moving, and she needed someone to help her. Ernie and I offered his car and his time for Sunday morning. Then we were going to drive to Josephine's house in Oceanside to deliver the Seagram's fabric and spend some time with Josephine and her family. Saturday, we had to ourselves, and we went swimming, to dinner, and to watch a fight that night on HBO. It was something Ernie really enjoyed, and I just hung around and sat with him. When the fight was over, I wasn't tired, so Ernie went to bed while I continued to watch TV. The most shocking thing was flashing across the screen. Princess Diana had been killed. The car had rammed a wall and she was declared dead.

I was stunned like the rest of the world, and we talked the next morning with Lauri at breakfast about how sad we felt. It was not a pleasant way to begin the day, but everyone was speculating about her death. Yet, we had things to do, and we knew we had to begin early and focus on them or we would never finish. We tried to put Princess Diana's death aside and proceed. Lauri actually shared some funny stories about her rehearsal, and we were in good spirits when we started. The move took about three hours, and we left Lauri in her new apartment with all her boxes to unpack. She thanked us, and we went on our way to repack Ernie's pickup truck with bolts of Seagram's fabric. He loved his pickup truck because he could transport things easily, and it had not cost him a lot of money. Being in construction and working on his house, he was always moving something around. He often took me shopping for merchandise for the store, and everything easily fit into the back of the truck. His help and support was unconditional. It had become a glue that bound me to him in a positive way.

Josephine lived near the shore, and Ernie wanted to stop at the beach, but I said it would be better if we went to Josephine's first and got that out of the way. Then if we had time later, we could take a walk on the Long Beach boardwalk. It wasn't easy finding Josephine's place, but once we were there, she couldn't have been more gracious. Her husband and Ernie piled all the fabric into one of Josephine's SUVs and then we sat around the living room sharing stories. Ernie talked a little bit about his childhood in Cuba, and Josephine told us about her Italian family. We laughed and relaxed, and she ordered a six-foot hero sandwich for everyone to eat for dinner. I thought to myself how Ernie must have felt eating something like that because when he was growing up in Cuba, his mother had to line up in the morning just to get a small amount of bread. I marveled at how far along in his life Ernie had come living in the United States. I hoped he was enjoying himself.

When we could no longer eat all that Josephine had, we discussed the Seagram's project, and Jo and I hammered out a fair price for her work. I wanted to charge Andy an honest price as well because I thought he had been overpaying for some of his premium gifts. We speculated that the bags we needed would take approximately one month to finish and that could give us just enough time to get them to Andy before a Christmas delivery. We packed the leftovers that Josephine wanted us to take, and then we were on our way. Although we were near the water, I did not want to go to the beach as it was near dusk. In an hour it would have been dark, and we were in an area that I was not familiar with. Ernie and I agreed that the following weekend we would drive to the Jersey Shore and spend a quiet day walking on the beach, but that night, I wanted to get right home as we both had to be up early the next morning. Ernie had to show his rental home to some people who were interested in buying it, and I needed to be at the shop by 10:00 a.m. Even though it was Labor Day, we were expected to be open all day, and I was the only one who could work. As the owner of the business, I handled a lot of the holidays. This was one of the busiest days at the store so I did not mind working. I just wanted to be rested and refreshed.

Once we got home, both Ernie and I fell asleep immediately. The strain of watching Princess Diana the night before had taken its toll. We were both exhausted. Ernie, however, popped up at 4:00 a.m. as if he were going to work. On construction jobs that was when he arose, and his body was accustomed to being ready at that hour. I was an early riser also, but that was a little too soon. I glanced at him through nearly closed lids and said, "Stay a while. It is still dark. You do not have to be there until 10:00 a.m."

He looked down at me from the side of the bed and said, "I'm okay. I'm awake and I want to do a little work on the house before they come."

Maybe I was uneasy because of Princess Diana, but I did not

want him to leave at that time. I tried to persuade him, but his mind was made up. I got out of bed, put on a robe, and walked him to the door. He had his little overnight bag, and he told me not to worry if he didn't call me that day because he was going to be busy with potential clients. I also had the store to run, so he said, "We will talk tomorrow."

We hugged and I kissed him good-bye. I was still very sleepy, but I walked to my window to watch the pickup truck emerge from the garage and to see his hand come up on the left side to wave good-bye. Then I felt comfortable enough to go back to bed.

The store was busy as I expected, and I went home happy with what I had earned. The next day, Avé was in the shop, and I kept busy with a new project. On Thursday of that week, I was going to a meeting at FIT (Fashion Institute of Tech) to be a part of a committee to make recommendations to the New York City public schools about their arts curriculum. It was an honor to be chosen to do this, and a client who was also a principal in the school system had recommended me. The meeting would run all day, and I wanted to write down my ideas about the kinds of collage work students might learn. I thought I might hear from Ernie that evening, but there was no call.

On Wednesday, I went to the shop all day with Avé as it was matinee day. Two people needed to be there to handle the rush. I stayed through the end of the day and still had not heard from Ernie. Thursday morning, I called and there was no answer. I called his beeper number as well and left my number. Neither one of us had cell phones then, so the beeper was the best way to reach him. By the end of the day, I was concerned. Even though we did not speak every day, three days without a phone call was unusual. I thought if something had happened at work, someone would have called me. If he were in the hospital, he would have made sure a friend would have called me. Since his family was in Cuba and his older aunt was the only one here and she did not speak English, I assumed it would be a friend. But I had heard nothing.

Friday, I tried again. No answer. By the end of the day, I decided I would call his friend Hiram and see what was happening. I dialed the store at about 3:00 p.m. and was talking to Avé about some jackets when our second line rang. Jenelle, who was our intern, answered the phone and said someone was asking to speak with me, that it was important. I told Avé to take the call, and I would wait on the line. There was silence, and then I heard Avé scream, "No, No, No. I can't. No. Jenelle come here. I have to leave."

Then there were muffled sounds. I could not hear anything else. I yelled into the phone, "Avé!" I thought something had happened in her family. I was very concerned. She finally came to the phone.

"I'm coming over. I have to talk to you."

I started screaming, "Is it Ernie? What is going on? Is he okay? Is he dead?"

I don't know where those last words came from, but I knew. I don't know how I knew, but I did. It was over. Avé was coming and I sat there in a daze. *I just knew....*

☙

Death sneaks up on you without warning, totally unexpected and sometimes vicious in its manner.

"Grandpa, Grandpa."

Someone screamed.

He was on the ground in the middle of the street. Dad was bending over him. There was blood under Grandpa's head. We were supposed to be going to the country for a holiday weekend. It was hot. The sun was bright. The traffic had stopped.

"Daddy," I yelled. "What's wrong with Grandpa?"

Someone took my shoulder and gently pushed me to the side. I looked at my dad. The sound of an ambulance was near.

"Don't touch him," I heard.

I turned away. Had Grandpa tripped? Did he hit his head? Was he going to be all right?

What had started out as a glorious adventure was becoming a nightmare. My father was pale. "Janie, go inside. Find your mom and Aunt Lillian and wait there. I'll be back soon."

"But Dad—" I started to say.

"Go, Janie. I'll be all right."

But nothing was all right. My grandpa was dead and it happened right in front of me, and there was nothing I could do to make it better.

...Helplessness. I was eight years old again.

ℭℨ

Avé arrived at my house and she had been crying. I hugged her and we sat down. Ernie had been killed in a car accident. It happened Monday morning when he was driving home from my apartment. Suddenly and without warning...just like Grandpa. He was involved in a head-on collision on I-78 W with a drunk driver going in the wrong direction in the left lane. His neck was broken, and he had not been wearing his seat belt. He died at the scene. Those were not her exact words, but that was what happened—a drunk driver, no seat belt, head-on collision. That could not be. Ernie was one of the most cautious drivers I knew. There was no way he was not wearing his seat belt. He always wore it. Something was wrong. This could not have happened. But it did. And all I could do was sit there and cry.

ℭℨ

From my journal early after Ernie's death:

Is it true that we have to always look over our shoulder for the pain? I cannot imagine just sailing along the way we were. How divine it would have been to grow old like that—finding amusement in each other, laughing at the silliest things and enjoying the peace and quiet of silence. How lucky we would have been to have had that....

The Impact of Death

When Avé had to go back and close the shop, she called my friend Annie Santiago, who came over to console me. I have only vague recollections of that time as I was in total shock. I know my friends Paul Antonelli, who was the music director at *All My Children,* and his partner Paul took me to dinner along with Annie and Avé. The most memorable moment of that night was a phenomenon I had never experienced before—flickering lights over our table. We had eaten at that restaurant many times and that night was the *only* time the lights flickered, and we were at the only table where it occurred. I have since learned that this phenomenon can occur when a soul is passing over into the next life and is contacting loved ones. Paul knew about this and told us that Ernie was trying to reach us. I did not believe him then, but now that I have read literature on after-death experiences, I do.

Avé stayed with me that night and the next. After that, my friend Lauri Landry came. I did not want to be alone. I kept expecting the key in the door to turn and Ernie would be there. Everywhere I looked in the apartment, I saw him. It was not until Avé had a "dream sequence" with him that I actually believed he was gone. She had been sleeping at home when she awoke suddenly, startled and in a daze. What had just happened? She looked around but nothing moved. Why was she so uneasy? She went to look in the mirror. Her eyes were bloodshot, her hair totally mussed, and her head ached. She could not remember anything—and then it came to her—Ernie had been there.

She had not seen him physically, but she had sensed his presence.... It was a telepathic vision. They were in the foyer of my home and he was imploring her, "Don't be afraid. Tell Jane that I am all right." He needed me to know that before his spirit could rest. There were tears in her eyes when she told me this, and we cried together. Although it was a relief to hear that he was all right, my soul ached because it meant he was really gone. It was time to accept that I was alone.

ഐ

The impact of Ernie's death was far reaching. The benefit was a little more than a month away and my mind set was gone. The lease on the Marriott store was up. Ernie had been set to retire, and we had planned to spend the winter in Florida. I was in the process of negotiating the lease at the Marriott and looking for a store on Las Olas Boulevard in Ft. Lauderdale. Although Mom's leukemia was in remission, Dad had been very ill with congestive heart failure, and I had counted on Ernie being around to get me through when Dad passed. I was a mess.

What was I going to do? All these people were depending on me to finish the benefit. My family needed me, and I still needed to earn a living and run a shop. Ernie's family in Cuba needed me. I had so many obligations. I had to finish the Seagram's project. And I had to renegotiate my lease in New York because I did not want to move to Florida by myself. I had to be able to handle all these decisions when inside I was falling apart.

I relied on my wonderful committee to get me through the fundraiser, and my friends helped as well. But "my heart" was not in anything. Although the event was a blur, I do know it went well. I remember Craig Rubano singing "Empty Chairs and Empty Tables" from *Les Miz* (as I had requested), and I remember breaking down. Neil Berg did a teaser concert with wonderful Broadway performers of his new musical *Prince and the Pauper*, and Christiane Noll, who played Emma in *Jekyll and Hyde*, sang beautifully to Robert Cuccioli. The room was full, and I remember standing between Walt Willey and Robert Cuccioli and shaking as I handed the Shining Star Award to Robert. Walt held my arm, and we thanked everyone, and Bob, who had gotten off a plane from California just to come to the event, sang "This is the Moment" from *Jekyll and Hyde* for his fans, and the night was over.

Where was I? Who was at the event? I do not even remember much, but I have wonderful pictures showing how happy everyone was. It was my first event without Ernie, and I don't think my parents were there either because Dad was too ill to travel. But we did it, and I felt a great sense of accomplishment and was grateful to my committee. They pulled it off.

1997 After Ernie

The year that Ernie died and the following one were the most difficult times in my life. I had rebuilt my life when I met Ernie and now I had no cushion, nobody to call a best friend who listened without judgment and had enormous pride in my accomplishments. Although, in many ways, Ernie was true to his Latin heritage, he was not macho in our relationship. He did not care if I was achieving some modicum of fame with the Leukemia Society event and my designing. Rather, he was proud to be able to help. He would look for things to sell in the store and accompany me to other galas the society held. He enjoyed watching the performers and liked going backstage to say hello to the celebrities. I always thought it all was such a thrill for him because of where he grew up and how hard life was for him in Cuba. He never forgot his family struggles, and he always found ways to send money to his mother and his brothers. I thought about how devastated they must be now that he was dead.

I did reach them in Cuba and bring his brother here to try to settle the estate because Ernie died without a formal will. We were not married or officially living together, so I had no claim on the estate. I thought it important that his brother make his claim, and through lawyers and much time and effort, Julian came here to work things out. I felt much better knowing I had done what I could to help them even though it was a strain on me financially.

I did think it was what Ernie would have wanted.

Over time, I went through many emotions regarding his death. I even got angry at him for leaving me in the middle of our lives, and I was furious that he wasn't wearing his seat belt. But if he was hit head-on and had been wearing one, he might have been paralyzed, and I know he would never have wanted to live that way. Acceptance was something I had to learn to find, and I went to a bereavement group for young widows and widowers. It was my wonderful friend, Dr. Perlow, who recommended that I try and talk to someone, and this group helped me to understand about death and loss, and coming back. For me, Ernie's death was only the beginning of the losses in my life, and I sank to the depths before I had the courage to try and pull myself out.

Renegotiating with the Marriott was a huge headache because although I expressed a desire to renew my lease, the hotel management wanted a large rent increase. This I could not afford. Had I been able to go to Florida with Ernie as I planned, it would not have even been an issue, but as it was I had to stay in New York and keep my shop. It was my main source of income, and I needed some stability in my life. Believe me, if I could have run away, I would have. The responsibilities I had toward the Leukemia Society and the store kept me rooted in New York.

In addition to my professional struggles, my father was slowly losing his battle with congestive heart failure, and I wanted to be as strong as I could for my mother. But I was not strong. I cried every day. I hid in my house or I went out to shows every night. I could not design. I left Avé to run the shop. I did not know what to do.

When it came time to discuss the lease, I remember putting on one of my best suits and insisting I see the General Manager and the Resident Manager at the Marriott to discuss my lease. That afternoon, I went to a meeting with them and told them my predicament (which I think they already knew). They looked at me with a little sympathy and told me they had already decided that all they could extend the lease for was one year, and I would have to pay a monthly increase for that time. I just sat there and stared at them.

"What about through January 2000 so I could be there for the millennium?" I asked.

"That would not work as we have to find a new tenant."

I knew the hotel would be packed in 2000 because it was a new century and everyone would want to be in Times Square for New Year's Eve.

"No, not negotiable." was their reply."

I felt like crying, but I was not going to do that. I said, "Thank you," and got up and left. Richard Morse, the Resident Manager came after me and said he'd have the extension of the lease ready for me to sign in a few days. "Thank you," I said again courteously and left.

The experience shook me, but I knew it was a business decision, and I could not afford to pay what they felt the lease was worth. It was another huge defeat. I would have to find a new place to work and earn a living. Where would I go? On top of all this, I had the Seagram's project to finish. What should have been my best financial year, and the happiest time of my life, had become the worst time.

Somehow the Seagram's order was finished on time, shipped, and paid for. Without that money, I do not know what I would have done because I was not paying any attention to the shop. Even though I finished my order and Andy was pleased, I had no interest in my business or anything else.

Life be damned, I thought. *I'm going to lose everything.*

And I almost did....

CB

I still had obligations to the Leukemia Society. Everyone was very kind to me, but I know they wanted me to continue fundraising. In a way, that was good because it kept me in touch with all the people on my committee, and I also had another British Airways event to plan for the spring. There were some wonderful people around me then, and one of the daytime actresses I had met, who had become my friend, really helped me. Louise Sorel, who played Vivian on *Days of Our Lives*, and I often had dinner. She had introduced me to Paul Antonelli. He along with his partner became my friends "the Pauls," who were rocks for me. And Annie Albarian, "little Annie" and Ilene and Abbey—they all tried to keep me busy. Through all the meetings and dinners and shows, I was there physically, but inside I was dead. Nothing could help ease the real emptiness when I went home.

Then it was February. Winter had descended on the city, and I never wanted to go outside. One day Jennifer Bassey, who played Marian Colby on *All My Children*, phoned me out of the blue. We had met a few times, and she had been wonderful about doing my events. She told me she had just heard about Ernie and wanted to express her sorrow. We chatted for a while and she said, "I know this sounds crazy, but I know someone who might help you."

I could not imagine what she was talking about.

"This woman helped me," she said. "And I'm sure since Ernie died suddenly, he is still around you. Just call Maureen and talk to her."

"What does she do?" I asked.

"Just call her and let me know how things go."

I could not imagine how a woman I did not even know could help me, but the next day, I contacted her. She said Jennifer had told her I would call, and she said she could help me reach Ernie. I did not know what she was talking about.

"What do you mean reach him? He is dead," I exclaimed a little impatiently.

"I know," she replied quietly, "but his spirit is still here."

Having always felt spiritually aware in life, I wanted to know more.

"When people pass over, there is a time period when they can still be reached. I believe Ernie would want to talk with you, and I can be your conduit to that world."

I was silent for a while and she started asking me questions about him. She even described him to me. It was her description of his eyes that reached me as he had almond-shaped eyes that were slanted and almost Asian looking and that was the first thing she said. *How could she know that?*

"We use the telephone and you call me. I'll have the room set. We will try and reach him. When the session is over (It usually lasts an hour.), I will have a tape to send you once you have mailed me your check." She paused. "Is this something you want to do?"

I could not speak. This sounded unreal. I would do anything to actually say good-bye to him.

"Then prepare some questions to ask him," she replied, "and I will talk to you Sunday morning at 10:00 a.m."

My channeling Ernie became a source of great comfort through that year. I really believed she had the gift and that I was talking to him. I know it sounds illogical, but there was no way she knew the things she did without being able to communicate with him. I began reading books about crossing over and the other side. She truly helped me understand what I had experienced, and between the channeling, the bereavement group, and the force of my charity work, I physically made it through that year. But the hits kept coming.

1998

Jackie Zeman & Douglas Sills

*I*n February, I decided to put some more effort into my shop. Avé and I wanted to have a New York-themed Valentine's Day display in our window. We bought beautiful red heart-shaped pillows, along with our vintage jewelry, and placed them to create a romantic window display. I actually had a few moments of inspiration at that time and began to feel a little comfortable with creating again. I knew Laurie Beechman had been very ill, but I hadn't expected her to pass when she did. She had been full of life and I admired her courage in fighting ovarian cancer. I secretly hoped against the odds that she would win her battle. It was not to be. She died that winter and it sent my depression deeper. I went to her funeral in Philadelphia and to her memorial in New York. My tears were just beginning. I listened to her *Listen to My Heart* and *No One is Alone* CDs all the time. I kept saying just one more time. I'll hear her voice just one more time. But once just didn't seem to be enough. I kept on playing them.

In March, the woman who sold and represented my special art to wear pieces, Marsha, passed away while watching television. She did not suffer as she had a massive heart attack and was gone. Not only was I losing friends, but now another person who nurtured my source of income was no longer around. How was I to recover? It is so difficult to find good sales people that I thought my business would never be the same. Marsha had been larger than life, over the top, always shooting for the moon.

"Why shouldn't Cher have your shawls?" she would say.

She would carry bags of one-of-a-kind Jane Elissa items everywhere she went. She was very encouraging to me about my art, and she often lectured me about being more confident and sure of myself. I loved her laugh and her exuberance and enthusiasm. Now that was quiet. Part of me just wanted to die.

On May 1, I was walking in the park, and I sat down at noon just to breathe the air of the green trees. The end was coming for my dad. The night before, I had spoken to the doctors and to my brother, who stayed in Florida to comfort my mother. I could not face going to see Dad. He looked frail, and they had to strap him down to the bed so he would not pull out the tubes. This once vibrant, jovial man was just a shell. I could not face him. So I talked to him in the park at noon and prayed for an easy and safe passing. I took comfort in knowing that he would be free of suffering and hopefully in a safer place. I just wanted him to be at peace, and I felt he would be. There was no way, however, that I would was going to be at peace for a long time.

ᛒ

Although I was dead inside, I still had an event to plan and that year our honorees were amazing people. I found a kindred spirit in Jackie Zeman. I was fortunate to meet her at a time in my life when her positive personality was really sunshine to me. She had lost someone in her family to leukemia, and she understood the commitment I had to eradicating the disease. I reached out to her through the Leukemia Society, and we had a meeting at the Marriott while she was in New York. I told her she was to receive the CMVRA for her charity work and commitment to the cause and what a huge fan of hers my mother and I were. After all, we had been watching *General Hospital* for what seemed like forever. The Luke and Laura story line was the biggest thing in daytime, and I was planning an event with Luke's sister—Bobbie Spencer. Moreover, she wanted to do whatever she could to help us.

Jackie agreed to participate in the small fashion show we would have that year, and when she saw our designs, she fell in love with my work. She chose what she wanted to wear, and I ended up giving her some new Jane Elissa designs. She looked fabulous in my creations as she was thin, but not emaciated, and she had great fashion sense. She knew how to put accessories together with our clothes. The Victorian apparel appealed to her, and over the years, she has either purchased or been given many of our designs.

Because of her commitment to Leukemia research, Jackie became an integral part of my events. She often came to New York to either be the committee chair, honorary chair, or just lend her name. We started to talk as Jane and Jackie over the years and developed a unique friendship. I have always felt we could talk about anything, and when I was emotionally down, her contagious laughter would keep me going.

One year, she came to our shop and we had lunch. She had never seen my artwork, and she admired what I was doing. After she left, I told Avé I wanted to send her the painting she really loved. She had said it would fit perfectly in her house as there was an English Victorian garden around a Tudor house. I had never seen Jackie's home, but I was sure she had beautiful taste. After all, her place was in Malibu by the ocean.

We packed the painting, shipped it that day and did not really focus on it again as we were busy preparing for a trade show. About a week later, we received a phone call in the shop from Jackie. She was screaming about how amazed she was to open the box and find that picture. She could not say enough nice things. I just told her it was a gift from my heart, and I knew it had found the right home.

I was lucky enough recently to go to California for the Romantic Times Convention and spend time with Jackie. I had introduced her to Carol Stacy from *Romantic Times Magazine* when she had come to New York to attend a women's expo, help

Sean McDermott, Jackie Zeman,
Jane & Carolyn Hennesy

me promote my "Hats for Health," and raise money for the LLS. Carol had suggested that Jackie might want to be a judge for the Mr. Romance contest at the convention and do a workshop with some other Los Angeles soap stars. Although Jackie hadn't written a book, Carol suggested she might want to and gave her some leads as to whom might work with her.

I thought this would be a good opportunity for Jackie to meet fans and possibly embark on another venture. But the nicest part of being in California and seeing Jackie was being invited to her home. This was her private space, and I was honored to be her guest. I brought Avé as we were working in Los Angeles, and my friend Perry was there to see his daughter. He drove us but no pictures were taken. It was a personal visit for me and was just about sharing lunch. I learned that I was right—Jackie has fabulous taste. Although she had downsized after her divorce, her home was magnificent. It also was in Malibu and as she said, "I live with Jane Elissa." I actually saw my painting, a screen we made for her, pillows and other pictures prominently featured. I wanted to cry. She told me how she wakes up every morning overlooking the ocean and staring at the English Tudor house in my painting. All I could do was hug her and say thank you for being in my life.

cs

The year that Jackie received the CMVRA, we had decided as a committee to honor Douglas Sills with the Shining Star Award. He was starring in *The Scarlett Pimpernel*, and he was absolutely charming. Douglas was tall, with brownish blond hair, sharp brown eyes, and a terrific wit. He was talkative and friendly, and I must confess I had a secret crush on him. When I approached him to be our shining star, he was gracious enough to accept the honor and worked diligently to make the event a success. Although he had never heard of the award, he knew what it meant to be an honoree and wanted to help the charity. Later, Douglas told people that "I flounced into his dressing room with all my charm and somehow cajoled him into accepting the award." But in truth, no performer deserved it more than he did that year. He was astounding every night he preformed on stage. He would improvise and entertain the audience with his comedic timing. I had seen the show at least twenty times, bringing new people with me, and each night was different.

I remember how committed Douglas was. We spent the day before Yom Kippur eve at his New York apartment talking about his life and the people we needed to contact to come to the benefit. His partner Todd would put together "the Douglas segment," and I worked on the fashion show. By then, we had Overland Entertainment to help us produce the event, and it had taken on a more professional flavor. People were coming back year-to-year, and we, as a committee, started to feel like we were making an important contribution. Not only were we getting the daytime celebrities who had been the mainstay of the event, but we were now attracting Broadway audiences.

The new magazine *In Theater,* as well as other publications, covered us. Even though Douglas was a dream to work with, I felt a lot of pressure. I did not want to disappoint the audience, my committee, or the Leukemia Society. So many people were now involved. This lovely little fashion show for leukemia had turned into the Jane Elissa Extravaganza, and I was the face of Jane Elissa. It was becoming a heavy load to carry.

Jane & Douglas Sills

The End of An Era

*A*t the end of December 1998, we moved out of the shop. I do not think I was ready for the move, but how could anyone be ready to leave a place that they loved and were successful in? The store had been a *must see* stop for tourists from all over the world. Avé and I had met people who became collectors of our work and had made some genuine friends there. My parents had stayed at the Marriott when they came to New York, and both Mom and Dad

Allan and Charlotte Meyers
(Dad & Mom)

worked the store. Dad would sit down on the sofa cutting out appliqué from different fabrics while my mom would regale customers with her tales of her modeling days and her genuine love for fashion. All the ladies for matinee day were in the same age range as my mother, so she also had a fan club. I think those days kept her young and gave her the strength to continue her battle with leukemia.

ɔʒ

How sad I felt that my dad was no longer with us. Where was I going? So many memories. How could I continue to put events together without space for people to try on outfits? I would have no base anymore. I could not go back to bringing people into my home. It would be so humiliating to do that. I thought I had taken steps forward, and suddenly I was nowhere. My self-esteem level fell really low.

I sat in the middle of my empty store, and I looked around thinking about the upheavals in my life. I also remembered how wonderful the ride had been. I saw Thorsten Kaye and Bob Woods clowning around one evening in my shop, trying on all kinds of wildly printed shirts to get ready for fashion shows.

They were poking fun at everything, but in a kind and loving way. I remembered Scott Bryce and Brooke Alexander changing in the back room and choosing their outfits. Brooke was such a classy person that she came with me to do an event on

Thorsten Kaye, Jane & Robert S. Woods in Jane's Shop

Channel 11 for leukemia, and Scott later married Jodi Stevens, who had become a friend during the time she starred in *Jekyll and Hyde*. I remembered Nathan Fillion, Tuc Watkins, and Christopher Douglas coming into the shop at the beginning of their careers on *One Life To Live* to try on clothes. No one laughed harder than they did. Tuc was very quick-witted and glib, and he made everyone laugh. Nathan was a close second, but Christopher Douglas was very shy, and I knew he was not as comfortable in the outfits they were going to wear.

"Ah, c'mon," I remembered Tuc saying, "It's for charity." Everyone laughed.

Only I was not laughing anymore. It was the end and as much as I wanted to cry right there in that space, I turned the lights off, held my head high, and closed the door for the last time.

It was over.

Transition

January was a very difficult month. Besides the darkness and cold of the winter, I felt my life was a reflection of the outside. I did not know what direction my life would take. When I learned I could not renew my lease, I started looking for a new space. My finances were tight, and I did not know if any store in my neighborhood could bring me the income the Marriott had. The large new stores were way over my rental budget, and the smaller stores were usually in an out-of-the-way location.

There were gaping holes in my life at that time. My father and Ernie were both gone. The store was gone, and my sales rep and Laurie were gone. It took all my strength to get up in the morning, but I forced myself. I decided that I must have had more things to accomplish. That was why I was still around. Sometimes I thought I was just rationalizing everything. I think we try to make ourselves as comfortable as we can in our world, but tragedies do change a person. Even if the spaces are filled, things are never the same.

Not a day went by where I didn't think about my losses. I remembered the drive and will that I had before to accomplish things, and I realized that was gone. At that moment, I was not even sure if I wanted to continue in my artistic endeavors. But I learned something very important from the experiences—the drive of talent always pushes on. Creativity may take a short holiday, but it never goes away. And that artistic spark has always been the driving force of my life. I just had to *want* it to come back.

While I had been investigating stores to rent, I was lucky enough to meet Perry Galimidi. He was the real estate agent for some new stores and apartments in a building that was under construction near my house. Although I did not rent his store, we became friends and have remained so. He helped me find people to renovate the 46th Street shop I would eventually rent. When we were finally ready to open, I felt confident that I had created a unique space in the neighborhood. I hoped that foot traffic would at least defray the rent costs while the profit would come with rebuilding the wholesale business. Being on a side street (46th) rather than an Avenue (like 9th Avenue) was a disadvantage, but we were only a few blocks away from the Marriott with the theater district on one side and the Intrepid on the other. I had to hope people would find us.

We officially moved to our store the summer of '99. I had left cards at the Marriott gift shop in case people were looking for us, and I told everyone I knew there where we had moved. I signed up for wholesale trade shows, and I started redesigning items in my "Remembrances of Romance" collection rather than concentrating on only New York tourist items. Since in the interim I had been working out of my home, it was a pleasure to finally have a different workspace. I know people think it is great to work at home, but there are down sides. Your work never leaves you. I could be sleeping and an idea would come into my head, and I would force myself to get up to play with appliqués so I could be ready to work in the morning. Going to the supermarket across the street was a big treat because I rarely went out otherwise. When the phone didn't ring, it was heaven.

Now, I wouldn't have to worry. Avé could run the shop and our young interns from the school could do more work. I felt an enormous sense of relief. The trouble was—there were no paying customers. There were lots of local people who were thrilled to see a store in the neighborhood, but no one was spending money. This was not a good sign.

Change of Venue

$\mathcal{T}$he LLS was looking for a new venue for their annual sports dinner. They had been contacted by someone from the Roosevelt Hotel located across town from the Marriott on Madison Avenue and the east side. Not a modern hotel, it had a very Victorian feel to it. The wood paneling was dark cherry and the colors were earth tones—greens, beiges, browns, peaches, etc. The rooms had floral décor and they felt very cozy. The banquet manager, however, had previously worked at the Marriott and knew of the Jane Elissa events. He invited me and Kerri Dubler to meet with him and listen to his proposal for our fundraisers. Kerri suggested we go and arranged a meeting.

Although I loved working with the Marriott, I needed a break from the memories I had there. The shop was gone, Dad was gone, Ernie was gone. My inspiration was gone. Sometimes it's just time to walk away. So when Mike treated us to lunch, showed us around, and gave us a complete proposal (including complimentary services, large discounts for guests, goodie bags, etc.), Kerri urged me to make the change and recognize new possibilities. We accepted.

The two large benefits we had in the years 1999 and 2000 at the Roosevelt Hotel featured some of the most well-known soap stars and the finest Broadway talent. The focus started to shift from the fashion show because without the Marriott location to

189

have fittings in, it was difficult to get the stars to come to our 46th Street shop. The photographers for the daytime magazines loved the fashion shows because there were always wonderful color shots to use in print, but it was an enormous amount of work to put together. Then, if we did work at the 46th Street shop, we had to bring all the fashions, prizes, signs, and auction items to the Roosevelt Hotel and that was not an easy task without a car. Somehow we managed, but I knew that I did not want to keep this arrangement beyond the year 2000.

In 1999, we chose Rob Evan from *Jeykll and Hyde,* to be our Broadway honoree, and Walt Willey was chosen to receive a lifetime commitment award. I cannot say enough about how generous Walt had been over the years. He gave of his time endlessly for every one of the benefits. And his friendship was something I cherished. He befriended my mother as well and always asked about her. He spent time with Meaghan and gave her the encouragement to follow her heart. We even went to his home in New Jersey to do a photo shoot and a mock birthday party for Meaghan. He always made time for us, and I wanted the public to know the kind of person Walt was. Rob Evan and Walt had become friends, and I was happy that they were both being recognized in the same year.

Rita Salk and Leslie Penny were still doing publicity for the show, and I had grown close to both of them. Rita always had a positive way of looking at things and would prod me to push just a little further to make the event better. She even offered to represent me as a publicist, but I always resisted. I did not want to step out of the shadows. Looking back, I think I had a fear of being judged and noticed, and at the same time, I was making clothing and artwork that were both *very* noticeable. It seemed easier to hide behind the material creations than be judged for who I was.

Before the event, we set up a green room where the stars could eat separately from the attendees. There was usually a cocktail hour where people who bought the pricier tickets got a private meeting with the stars. Then, everyone went in to eat, bid on silent auction packages, look at items from a small Jane Elissa Boutique I had set up, and just mix and mingle with their friends. In 1999, Walt was in an exceptionally funny mood and he kept making jokes about a "lifetime" award going to people only when they're about to kick the bucket. Why were we honoring him? Was there something he didn't know about his health?'

"No, No, No..." I said over and over again. "People need to know what a great person you are."

"If they really knew me, they'd know better," was his reply.

Two people who *did really* know him and wanted to wish him well that evening were Kelly Ripa and Mark Consuelos. Although they could not attend the actual event, they came back into the green room to lend their support and visit with Walt. Kelly, who has always been gracious and accommodating, greeted us very warmly. Her husband Mark seemed tired, but I was happy they came, especially since they had been out all day attending something else. Their support pleased everyone.

Jackie Zeman had flown in from California just to be our honorary chair. She also modeled in the fashion show, and as always, looked beautiful in our clothes. Ron Raines, who had come with me to the Columbia Presbyterian Hospital to visit with children with cancer, received the CMVRA, and Cameron Mathison from *All My Children* gave Walt his Lifetime Achievement Award. Cameron had been a big supporter of our cause, and I was thankful he could come to recognize Walt.

Rob Evan was our shining star that night and he truly deserved it. He and Neil had helped me plan the musical portion for the event, and as usual, it was filled with Broadway talent. Rob had

Jane & Cameron Mathison

wanted me to present his award, and at first I refused. He insisted, though, saying that I was the one who had inspired him to do these charitable benefits. I had also taken Rob and Walt to the lab at Columbia Presbyterian to meet our first sponsored researcher—Erik Martinez Hackert. Rob spoke movingly about his visit to the lab and the hospital and what we learned about leukemia research. On the side of the stage, I listened and teared up. It was one of my memorable moments that night.

The event was successful, although not as financially lucrative as some. I knew I had to keep working harder to bring in more revenue.

CB

The next event was the year 2000, and I chose to recognize Linda Eder as my shining star. She had starred in *Jekyll and Hyde* with Robert Cuccioli and Rob Evan. Linda had a very distinctive lush voice. It was the closest I've ever heard to Barbara Streisand. I did not know how to reach her, but Rob helped us get to her people. For the first time, I actually did not have a personal sit-down with the honoree. Linda was married to Frank Wildhorn at the time (the composer of *Jekyll and Hyde* and *Scarlet Pimpernel*), and although I loved his music and wished I could speak with them, I was only permitted to talk to their people. I wanted to explain to them what the award meant and have them help us to reach the people they might want to attend, but talking to them was not an option. I think until they actually attended the event, they did not really understand our goals.

Luckily Jackie Zeman was the honorary chair again, and Annie Albarian was the event chair. Both of them understood what needed to be done to "sell out" the night, and they worked very hard to do it. Rob Evan, along with Neil, put together the musical segment to honor Linda's work, and I brought the daytime celebrities in for a short fashion show. Cameron Mathison received our CMVRA and so did Paul Antonelli from *All My Children*. It was a star-studded lineup.

Walt Willey was supposed to be the emcee, but he had to work late at the studio so we were left without a host. Luckily Rob Evan, who was going to handle the music segment, volunteered to host the entire event. Without him, I would have had no hair left. There was a lot of press that night, and Linda and Frank were seated at the head table. Because Rob knew her so well, he cajoled both her and Frank and their guests to banter back and forth with him. When it came time for the live auction, I think Linda realized the scope of the benefit and gave Rob extra prizes to auction off. The audience loved it.

When Linda received her award, she brought her own pianist to play for her. She had originally planned to sing only one song, but once she was on stage, she decided to give more of herself and sang three. There were so many "Jekkies" (fans of the show *Jekyll and Hyde*) in the audience that she received standing ovations after every song. She thanked everyone for coming and called me up to the stage to offer her thanks. Rob returned and the three of us thanked everyone for coming and told them to come again next year. Even as I stood on that stage, I wondered if I would have the energy for another event. Inside I felt a change coming.

David Hasselhoff

*W*hen we honored Linda Eder, *Jekyll and Hyde* had been rotating different stars in the lead role. Jack Wagner from *General Hospital* had tackled the part. Sebastion Bach, who I had gotten to meet and had truly a grand Broadway voice besides his rock voice, came next, and eventually David Hasselhoff finished the Broadway run of the show. Because our fundraiser was taking place right as David took over the part, we did not approach him to attend. It was right after or during his extremely successful run on *Baywatch,* and I think we thought he was a Hollywood personality who would be too big for our relatively small New York City Theater event. I was probably intimidated by his stature, as well. Linda Eder was a pop musical star, and she was coming. I was still thinking small. One thing I learned, think small, stay small. Think big, grow big—you move in the direction that you think. I'm not sure I've even applied that lesson to this day, but I am trying.

About a week after the event, I received a phone call from a young man. "Hi, I'm calling for Jane Elissa."

"Yes, this is she," I replied.

"I'm calling for David Hasselhoff. He would like to do something for the Linda Eder event."

Shock—could this person be for real?

"I'm sorry," I replied, "but the event has passed."

"Oh well, I'll tell David then."

"Wait a minute," I said. "Would David like to do something else?"

I don't know where that idea came into my head from, but somehow it did.

"What do you have in mind?"

I remembered that I had taken Walt and Robert Evan to the lab to meet the researcher I had sponsored, and I had also taken Ron Raines and Christine Toy Johnson to visit some of the children at Columbia Presbyterian Hospital.

Wouldn't it be great to take an international star to see the kids? I didn't know if he'd do it, but I thought it would be a really wonderful thing for him to do. "Perhaps he would like to come with me to visit some children who are cancer and leukemia patients at Columbia Presbyterian. I have sponsored a researcher there, and I think I could arrange a short visit."

"Well," he said, "I'll run it by David and call you back. Here is my number if you have any other information."

"Thank you," I said, and we hung up.

I had been standing by the phone, but after the call I sat down. *David Hasselhoff*, I said to myself. *Baywatch, Knight Rider*, California guy. *Did I really receive that call? It must have been my imagination.* But it wasn't because a few days later, his person called. (All celebrities have people who handle their lives; everything goes to the people first and then they get back to you.)

"David is very interested in meeting children. I will get back to you with the dates he is available. We think it's best before Christmas as the show will probably close early January, and David will be busy the last few weeks of December."

"Okay," I said. "Looking forward to hearing from you."

Click again. Now what? I had to call Erik to find out how to arrange this.

With Ron Raines, we had visited children in the playroom at the hospital. David wanted to go to the children's rooms to spend time with them one on one. I did not even know if that could be set up. Well, dream *big* and make things happen.

I called Erik, who called the head of the hospital, who called the head of the pediatric cancer unit, who called the head nurse, who called me.

"Ms. Meyers?"

"Yes."

"We can arrange a visit. Afternoons are best. Just let us know as soon as you can."

"Thank you."

"Bye."

It was going to happen. All I had to do was get the dates from David, and it would be set. Probably a weekday afternoon—a couple of hours. In and out quickly, but with time enough for each child. That would work perfectly.

"Hello, may I speak to Jane please?" said a female voice on the phone.

"This is she. Who is this?"

"This is Judy's office. Please hold."

I knew who it was. She had originally been Robert Cuccioli's publicist so I knew her well.

"Hi, Jane. How are you?"

We exchanged greetings but I wondered why she was calling.

"I just want you to know that I'm David Hasselhoff's publicist and his time is very limited."

"Oh," I said.

I didn't really want to deal with the details on the phone as she had been very gracious with Robert Cuccioli and me when he was in *Jekyll and Hyde*. I understood her concern, but I knew everyone would be so disappointed if he did not come. "Well, thank you for calling, Judy," I said. "Take care."

What to do next? Do I call David's person? Do I call his California office and plead? Do I let the whole thing drop? Or do I just wait to hear from them? I did nothing.

By late afternoon, I hadn't heard from anyone else. Was the visit dead? Was it never to happen? I could not wait any longer. I called *his person*—voice mail. I left a message to call me immediately. Then I called his California office and left the same message.

Nothing.

At about 8:30 p.m. that night, I got a phone call from his assistant. "Hi, Jane. Is everything okay?"

"Yes," I said, "but I received a phone call from Judy saying this visit wasn't going to happen."

"No, it is. David wishes to do it quietly without any publicity or attention. Is that okay?" he asked.

"Yes." I was thrilled. "That's exactly how I would want it."

"Okay. These are the dates he can be there."

I wrote them down and in two weeks we were there. I went up in a cab with a Leukemia Society volunteer, and we met with the head pediatric nurse in the cancer unit before David arrived. He did not ask to be picked up in a limo or for any other special treatment that celebrities usually get. I was very nervous because I think his celebrity stature intimidated me. But I was excited to be doing this for the children and the hospital, and also because David had requested it. That showed me that he really cared about the children.

We were supposed to be there around 3:00 p.m. and at 3:00 p.m., a yellow cab pulled up in the upper entrance to the hospital. Out came David's assistant, who I had never met, and then came David, dressed in his red *Baywatch* jacket. He was very tall and towered over everyone. He really was larger than life with that big California smile, white teeth, blondish brown hair and a beautiful tan.

"Hi, I'm Jane. Nice to meet you." I introduced the Leukemia Society volunteer and Susan, our escort from the hospital.

"Come in," Susan said, beaming.

They talked a while and I spoke with David's assistant. He told me David had two hours and he'd brought eight by ten photos for David to sign and give to the children. I thanked him and we all went up to the children's wing. People were staring in the hospital. I heard whispering. "Is that him? Is that really him?"

We all smiled. I posed with him by a giant bird at the

beginning of the tour, and the pictures were taken for our files and my personal use. (It is now on my website for all to see.)

David entered each child's room; parents, nurses, and staff came to mingle. Even though some of the younger children might not have known him, all the parents did. The cameras were flashing all afternoon. There were many hugs and private moments for him with the families. I was moved by how genuine he seemed with the children and how he asked the parents about each child and posed with them.

The two hours went by very quickly and his assistant reminded me that David had to leave because he had a show that night. I thanked him over and over and he said, "No big deal. Thank you for letting me come."

And then he was gone to find his own cab with his assistant. We all looked at each other—Susan, the Leukemia volunteer, the head nurse, and I—and smiled. David had been one of the most unselfish and gracious celebrities I'd ever worked with. He wanted no publicity, no attention, and no special treatment. That day was one of my most fulfilling celebrity experiences.

Jane & David Hasselhoff
at the Presbyterian Hospital

Michael James Madeo

$\mathcal{A}$s I walked home one night from dinner at the Roosevelt Hotel with Perry Galimidi, he pointed out the beautiful Safra Bank on the corner of Fifth Avenue and said wouldn't it be nice to have an account there. We peeked in the windows and saw chandeliers dripping with crystal, cherry wood desks, and antique-looking fixtures. The décor had a feeling of going to a sumptuous dining room rather than a bank. I decided I would open a small account with them.

Michael James Madeo was one of the managers, and I was lucky enough to have him call me to his desk. He was tall, blond, brown-eyed, and spoke with a British accent. I told him I fell in love with the bank from the outside, and he said he hoped I would like it better now that I was inside. I laughed and said it was even more inviting. I mentioned that I once had a store in the Marriott Hotel, and he told me that he and his mother had gone there and loved it. We immediately bonded. How could I not like this manager? He loved my work.

Over the next few years, Michael and I became the best of friends. I count him as one of the family. He has taught me about managing money and has shown me how to think more about growing my business in the future. Without his wisdom, I never would have gotten through those very lean years. With each twist, he helped me find a better way of doing things. I learned to stop making inventory that was not profitable and to concentrate on the items that were. He also established a credit line for me, which enabled me to buy goods as I needed to when I did not actually have the cash on hand. Even though Michael eventually left Safra Bank, I followed him to his new and more lucrative opportunities.

Eventually Michael became involved in my leukemia events. When I decided to scale down my fundraisers, he encouraged his present employer, Sterling National Bank, to be a sponsor. He became the chairman of the events and even had small fundraisers at the bank. We are currently working on a much larger project which will come to fruition this year. I have goaded him into being my co-chair and he has agreed. He is one of the biggest cheerleaders for Jane Elissa, and I am lucky to have stumbled on him in a bank of all places.

Aiden Turner, Jane & Michael James Madeo

Claire O'Connor

$\mathcal{R}$ita Salk always looked for new ways to promote my ventures. She was there for me as a friend and confidant. She pushed me to do more with my business, and whenever an opportunity appeared, she suggested I try it. At one point, she was contacted by another publicist, Claire O'Connor, who had heard about my events through British Airways. Claire was interested in helping out as well, but she had another agenda for me.

Claire had worked with rock 'n' roll royalty and nightclub impresarios. She was the publicist for the Limelight Disco in its heyday, worked with the Supper Club and Disco Rasputin in Brighton, Brooklyn and with the China Club where *all* rock 'n' roll stars, athletes, and celebrities went to relax. I was not sure why she contacted me, but Rita suggested I meet with her and see if we could expand our LLS audience.

The meeting with Claire was a delight. She was young, thin, blue-eyed with long dark hair, about average height with a thick, almost hoarse voice and a deep throaty laugh. She lived around the corner from me and was married to a rock musician. I asked her how she'd heard of me and she said her Russian client had met someone who had attended the first British Airways event and wanted me to do something like that for them at the Rasputin nightclub.

Where is this "Rasputin?" I remember asking.

"It's the hottest club in Brighton Beach, Brooklyn."

"So what can I do?"

She wanted me to meet Raiza who was the marketing person at the club and see what I could do. More importantly, Claire had a connection to the China Club, which had moved from Uptown into the theater district. There was something she wanted me to work on with them, but that would be later. I agreed to meet with Raiza and discuss the China Club after the Tenth Anniversary Gala of Jane Elissa and the completion of my Seagram's project for Andy. Unfortunately, my grief over Ernie's death put many of my plans on hold.

But Claire persisted. She told me over and over again that I needed something different in my life. She helped me arrange a birthday party for myself at Rasputin in January. I never would have done that without her. Yet, it was a lot of fun, and I was surrounded by people I loved and cared about. She encouraged me to do another televent for the Leukemia Society and get myself back into life. The next project she had for me was a huge endeavor, which I would have never undertaken had Ernie been alive. But I've talked about that space that we have in our lives that needs filling—at times more than others—and all I was doing was running from Broadway shows to movies, to more Broadway shows in an attempt to *fill* the emptiness. She wanted to put a time-consuming new project into that space.

Not the right time, I thought, but I would listen to her ideas.

Even though my knowledge of how to put together events had grown, I did not consider myself a "producer." I was called that by other people, but I did not realize that I was "producing" something. The elements that went into putting together a good show were like embellishing a canvas. There had to be color, it had to move around, there had to be blank space against mixed brilliant hues for contrast. The songs had to be interspersed with ballads, rock, and Broadway-belting anthems. People had to get involved. We needed humor and then serious revelations about the devastation of a cancer diagnosis. The balance between male and female actors had to be achieved, and the female audience had to have a little titillation—hence, some open shirts and no shirts under vests. One actor had even gone so far as to ask me to take a vest with no shirt away from another actor because his body was buffer than the first one. He said he worked at it and wanted to strut his stuff. The other actor didn't care so who was I to argue? As it turned out the fans *loved* it.

All these decisions I made or found other people to make were geared by a subconscious knowledge of design. I also had studied piano since I was five, and I think the fact that I knew I had to practice at least one to two hours a day helped me in later life to develop discipline and focus. I recommend that to anyone raising a child—give them something they must do on a daily basis that they ultimately will enjoy and progress at, whether it be music, sports, or the arts, etc. I think it sets the basis for having a focused life. At least it provides a tool for taking on future long range tasks. Production of something comes at the end. In some ways, I was now producing a piece of art, if only for a short time. It was not art for the wall, but the "art of the show" to be enjoyed for the moment and remembered in the future.

It was to be a producing job that Claire asked me to do for the China Club. She introduced me to Danny and Michael, who ran the club, and we discussed exactly what Danny wanted. He loved Broadway and wanted to do a "Broadway Series" on Sunday nights, which was a quiet night for the club and put on a cabaret show featuring Broadway stars. I would be paid from the proceeds for the night, and there would be a cover charge plus a food and drink minimum. They would do the publicity to get it off the ground, and I would find the talent and put the show together. I told them I needed a musical director and a piano player. Danny had someone in mind, but I wanted to bring in Neil Berg, who I had worked with for the past few years on my events.

"No problem," he said.

I felt comfortable with Neil as he played the piano and was familiar with everyone in the Broadway community. He was working on his own show *Prince and the Pauper*. If I was going to do this, I needed someone who could work with performers and also play for them. Neil was perfect.

I told Danny and Claire I would talk to Neil and get back to them. Neil thought it was a great opportunity to build something and also find new people to attend my events. He was anxious for me to take the job, and I had nothing else I wanted to focus on then, so I said yes. We would work together with Claire and Danny to get people out to hear music in New York City on a Sunday night in the summer when most of the time they were either in the Hamptons or at the Jersey Shore. This would not be an easy task.

I spent almost two years working on these nights with Neil and Claire. Sometimes, we would have standing room only, and other times, there were no more than thirty to forty people. The concerts that drew the most people were when we had more than one entertainer for the night. It seemed like people would come home from the beach if they could see a few current Broadway performers together. The more performers, the more ticket sales—but then the money was being split among more people. This was *not* a money-making job, and as time went on, I became more of the behind-the-scenes person and the greeter or hostess at the door than show coordinator. I would give comments, but I left it up to Neil to organize the talent. He liked it that way. This was his profession, and it gave him a tremendous amount of visibility in the theater community. We were working with Brian Stokes Mitchell, Douglas Sills, Alice Ripley, Brian d'Arcy James, Rob Evan—all top people headlining current Broadway shows. Even Catherine Hickland, from *One Life to Live* had her cabaret night at the China Club.

The club made money from drinks as we moved the show out of the dining room and onto the rock 'n' roll disco stage. Everyone was happier that way. We even presented a British Airways sponsored cabaret there. Danny Zolli, whose unusual voice brought the house down when he sang from *Jesus Christ Superstar*, La La Brooks from the "oldie" group the Crystals, and Michael Lanning from *Civil War* came to perform. Combined with singers from Smokey Joe's Cafe and Rob Evan, we had a magical evening. Neil and I had learned pacing and were producing terrific shows—at least the audience was happy and that made them more generous to the cause.

ᑭ

One of the positive offshoots of these shows was a new job for Neil. After Laurie Beechman's death, Andy no longer had a Broadway performer for his corporate concerts. Overland, the production company that had helped me with the shows, wanted to put a Broadway type show together for some of their corporate clients. They had specialized in rock 'n' roll, but they wanted something different. Lee Ann and Jonathan from Overland called me. I went to a meeting at their office, and they asked me for advice. They were thinking that Neil could put the Broadway performers together, and they could present this to their client. I told them it would be a great idea, and I spoke with Andy about it. He liked the thought of bringing a Broadway troupe to his corporate galas. Lee Ann said she would speak to Neil and thanked me for my help. She also asked at that time if I would work on something for a current client—Joe Grano from Paine Webber—for his birthday party in New Jersey. As a favor to Overland, I asked Neil if he would do something with three or four people for Joe Grano's party. Neil agreed and I put everyone together.

Neil worked on the party with Overland, and I attended with friends. Joe Grano and his wife were marvelous people. They so loved Broadway and appreciated the fact that top Broadway talent would be performing for Joe and his guests. I actually got to be backstage and then in the audience for a performance without having to worry about running back and forth to direct the show. For once I was a guest. I did feel proud, though, that I had gotten these people together. (Just an aside—Joe Grano has gone on to produce the *Jersey Boys* so his love of Broadway took him in a favorable direction.)

Overland was pleased that Joe was happy, Andy was happy, and Neil had a blossoming career on the corporate circuit. It was nice to know I had helped put that all together, but I received no financial remuneration. I did not see it as a business deal. I was simply helping friends.

The Billy Doll

*I*t was Claire O'Conner who would again challenge me with a new artistic project. She had been hired to publicize an event involving a special doll—it was the "Billy" doll. This doll was a very good-looking miniature version of an anatomically correct, well-endowed male. There was to be a special party held in Soho for the unveiling of a new version of the doll, and Claire was recruiting celebrities to come to the event (which was a benefit for an AIDS charity), and to design new clothes for the doll. Each doll would then be auctioned off at the event and the proceeds would go to the charity. Guess who she wanted to make a costume for the doll?—Jane Elissa—not Jane, the event producer; Jane, the artist. I had never made anything for dolls before, but our seamstress Nora loved making doll clothes, so here was her opportunity. Now we had something different to do, and I did feel a slight tingle creatively.

The evolution of the costume came through three people—Avé, Nora, and myself. I do not remember how we came upon our idea, but we ended up dressing Billy in an Americana outfit with a flag hat and a phantom of the opera-like cape with American and theater symbols. I guess I could not escape my penchant for the theatrical so Billy would be as bold as possible. It really was an honor to be asked to do this as some of the other people they asked were superstars like Elton John. I had no idea how much money my doll would go for, but because of the publicity in the fashion world, it seemed like a good opportunity.

I brought Paul Adent (who had become my designated escort). My friend, Paul Antonelli, did not mind if I borrowed his significant other on occasion. No one I know has a more amiable, friendly, and positive attitude than Paul Antonelli. Not only is he kind and loyal, but he and his partner, helped me immensely during the first months after Ernie's death. They would call me every day and come over to see me. They never let me be alone. They would call Charlotte, my mom, and entertain her on the phone. They helped me arrange my birthday party and encouraged me to grieve and not rush myself. Sometimes leaning on others is necessary, and I was lucky to have the Pauls.

I do not remember much about the event except that I posed next to my Billy Doll, which was featured in a revolving parade of other newly-dressed Billy dolls. There were mainly men at the event. Although they were more interested in meeting Paul than myself, I still managed to have some interesting conversations about fashion. The director of the event loved my doll and said he already had someone who wanted to buy it. Thank goodness. I did not want to be the only doll unsold. He also told me that people nicknamed the doll "Captain America" because there was a comic book character who wore an American cape. Little did I know that years later that character would be the star of a movie.

The day after the "Billy Doll" event, Claire called me and told me my doll was a huge hit and would probably be featured in some photo stories in the magazines. I gave my permission to use the photos, and I gave her some quotes about the making of his costume. Although I saw Claire after that project, she had moved on to more nightlife public relations, and I was easing back into being Jane Elissa, the artist/designer. We would catch up on the phone or see each other in the neighborhood, but we were not working together. I actually have a current project I was going to call her about, but I opened our newspaper and in the obituary section saw her name. I was shocked. She had just passed away from lung cancer at the age of fifty-one. Sadness overwhelmed me. Memories came back of that deep, hearty laugh and her encouraging words about moving on came into my head. I will always have her and her family in my prayers.

Transitioning Back

I felt dead. For many months during those years, I felt creatively dead. Although I worked on two events, coordinated the China Club Broadway Series, and opened the new shop, I was not earning enough money to carry my expenses. I was also running from "thing to thing" in an attempt to avoid facing the space. It seemed to the outside world that I was having a great time—shows, celebrities, magazine photos, Leukemia Board work—all just a means to cover the emptiness. Late at night, the space would greet me in my house and I would sob—on and on until I fell asleep. I thought about selling my apartment and disappearing somewhere. I thought that a lot—but I did not know where I would go. *Start a new life somewhere less visible*, I thought. *Something simple, quiet*—was that what I really wanted? I did not know.

My therapist had moved. My bereavement group was over. (Members were only allowed to stay one year.) My store was not doing well. My tenure on the Leukemia Board was nearly over. The *space* would become enormous—or would it?

Take a new step, I kept telling myself. Look outside yourself for new opportunities. Take away the anger, the pain, the sorrow, and let the joy back in. Look at all the wonderful things you are doing. Stop seeing them as a burden and start seeing them as a blessing. They are keeping you alive. Look again at the beauty around you and open the door, create, put those fabrics together, and make more art....

The creative spirit inside me was getting restless. It needed nurturing and I had not been ready. Slowly, however, I sensed the artistic voice coming back. How, why, I cannot answer—maybe I just wanted to be whole again.

☃

...Memories of Brooklyn wafted through the air.

Grandpa again—the carousel, the family, the Sunday afternoons.

And then the call came.

My heart would ache again....

It was the day before my birthday and I was at home thinking about the way my life was when the phone rang. It was my cousin Michael. He sounded awful.

"What is it?" I asked.

There was hesitation.

"Arnie died last night. He had a massive heart attack and went very quickly."

I dropped the phone and screamed. I just could not say another word. I could hear Michael talking, and I picked up the phone. "I'm sorry," was all I could say. "I will call you back."

There was silence with me. Arnie had been one of the most important people in my life. I adored him and worshiped him. He had been the oldest of my cousins, and I followed him and his brother Michael around like a little puppy.

This could not be true. Not another person gone in my life. I refused to believe it. But it was true. Arnie had passed and again I felt that pain.

I was tired...really tired and I felt so alone. Even with my friends around, the loneliness was from inside. I was sick of being pushed down and having to start all over again. I had lost so much before, and I had made every effort to manage the grief, pain, and losses. Now I felt as if I was at sea—drifting, drifting, drifting. I did not know where this would lead.

☙

I was not at home in the Roosevelt. As lovely as it was, I liked the proximity of the Marriott to my home, my current shop, and the theater district. The location right on Broadway was central to everything we did. I spoke to Carol Dickson, my friend, who ran the *One Life to Live* and *All My Children* fan club luncheons and had come with me to the Roosevelt. We decided if we were going to continue to do our events, we wanted to be back on the West Side. The Roosevelt prices had been less expensive, but the convenience of the Marriott overrode the disparity in price. Besides, there were a few newer places in Midtown that might work, as well. I decided to investigate the Hilton and Doubletree in Times Square. Before I had a chance to even make one phone call, my phone rang.

It was the office of the General Manager of the Marriott calling. When he spoke with me, he asked if I could provide some insight to the new vendor who now occupied my previous space as to the type of clientele which frequented the hotels. Although this man had created a beautiful, clean-lined shop, it was not as tourist friendly as ours had been. Without items under twenty and thirty dollars, it would be difficult for the average Broadway-loving New York City tourist to find something to bring home as gifts. I phoned the store owner and tried to explain to him that he needed a little more price variety in his shop. His answer to me was "I'm not going to make a grocery store." And I thought to myself, if you do not do that, you will be out of there in six months. And sure enough, that is what happened. It gave me no pleasure to see the store vacant because it had been my baby, and now it was abandoned. There was a sadness in me, which was soon replaced by apprehension.

When I had spoken to the General Manager, we had also discussed the possibility of the hotel gift shop buying some of my handmade New York merchandise. He suggested I meet with the manager of the store and see what could be arranged. She visited my place on 46th Street and asked me if I wanted to rent an area in the Marriott gift shop—it would be a small window space, which I could use to sell all my items—Jane Elissa designs, jewelry, tote bags, artwork, etc. It was the size of a walk-in closet, but it had window frontage, and I could separate it from their shop with a Jane Elissa designed screen behind the side walls—in essence closing it off when unattended. Although small, it would bring me back to a market I knew well and provide exposure to people who enjoyed our merchandise.

It was an opportunity to earn money again as the store on 46th Street had been a drain on my savings. The only problem seemed to be my emotional uncertainty about returning to do business in the Marriott. There were so many memories.... What convinced me to make the return was the old adage—you have to pay the rent—and I thought with my wholesale business growing and a "mini" store in the Marriott, I would have less of a financial burden and possibly start to earn money again. I also would have a little more leverage to get a good deal for my fundraiser if I had the mini shop, so I decided to do a month-to-month arrangement thinking it might lead to something long term. Ever the optimist, I was....

We kept the 46th Street store and created a *busy* two-by-four feet space at the Marriott. It was a little closet within their shop, and as usual, we had the most artistic and fun things I could design as well as other artists' creations. Everyone stopped to look in our window. And if they did not buy from us, they were at least in the gift store, and there was plenty for them to purchase. It seemed like a win-win situation.

The only complication came with the arrangement of our display. The Marriott feared that our window was too cluttered. I tried to explain that people loved it, and in order to make the rent and profit in such a small space, I needed a lot of merchandise. I had brought my extravaganza back to the hotel for that year, and my friend Carol and her fan clubs, who I had also taken to the

Roosevelt, came back with me. It would not have been prudent for them to ask me to leave, as I was bringing revenue to their gift shop, but I never felt secure.

Unfortunately, a new wrinkle appeared....

There was a disaster in New York—a worldwide nightmare. I lived forty blocks up the West Side from the World Trade Center, and I was actually on my roof when the second building was hit. I had no idea what was happening. I raced downstairs to watch TV as the horror unfolded. I refused to go into the Marriott that day to open my shop because I felt I could not make and take money on such a terrible day. The gift store did extremely well because people could not leave New York, but I did not want to be there. It was too painful.

The city was decimated. Morale was low but people bonded together. We had all shared a horrendous experience. I had seen from my roof the second plane hit the towers. I had watched bodies falling out, debris coming, fire emanating from the floors. Smoke smell penetrated my apartment even though we were over forty blocks away, and the air was still thick with dust. People walked up my avenue—tons of them—just to go home. My friend Michael and his friend Dean came over to watch what was happening on TV. All the business offices were closing, and they could not get home. The Long Island Railroad was shut down until the evening. We did not even know who Al Queda was—we were just stunned.

Tourism in New York fell after 9/11. The hotels were empty. Everyone was afraid of what could happen next. I did not feel that way as I had seen so much horror over the previous four years that I was able to offer comfort to people. Part of the grieving process is moving ahead. And I had taken those first steps. The people who did come to New York were very supportive of all the shop owners and wanted to give back to us so we could rebuild our business. My little space and even my 46th Street shop were busy. I made beautiful commemorative Trade Center pictures, and we sold a lot of New York, USA items. Since business was "off," I was encouraged to stay in my space at the Marriott. I am happy I did as I reconnected with many former customers who stayed in the hotel.

I worked very hard to make 2001 profitable. I did not do an October benefit because I knew no one would attend. I relied on my prior experience of loss to move forward with my life. I approached the banquet manager at the Marriott to do another October event the following year. New York's economy had slid down and the tourists were just not coming. I wanted to survive and thrive, but a desire to help New York and represent it positively to all the tourists kept me going.

Jackie Zeman said she would be the honorary chair for the next event which we would hold at the Marriott. Walt agreed to host and Rob Evan and Neil both said they would work on the musical part with me. We had lost many committee members as time went on because people have different agendas each year. Those who stayed with us—Loraine, Ilene, Paul, Jackie, and Annie Albarian—were truly committed to the charity. The rest of the people either were in my life for a short time or anxious to become best friends with the celebrities. When they realized that was not going to happen, they were no longer interested in participating. Some people volunteered to help backstage thinking they could meet the celebrities and not have to pay to attend the event. Susan from the LLS taught me that everyone paid—even those on the committee. A few people decided not to volunteer when they realized they could not come for free. It was always a learning experience, and sometimes I was fooled by how nice and interested someone appeared to be while actually wanting to date one of the singers. That was a *no-no*. In time, I weeded those people out.

Getting money from people for charity was difficult that year. People were being very cautious, and they still were not rushing to come back to New York. Ron Bohmer had just starred in a third version of the *Scarlet Pimpernel*, and he agreed to be our shining star. He had performed for us at three or four events, and he was a compelling performer.

I had seen him in *Les Miz* and loved him ever since. I also wanted to recognize both Marj Dusay and Jennifer Bassey, both from *All My Children,* for their devotion to the event and charitable contributions. Another person I wanted to recognize was Annie Albarian for her commitment to this event and her true friendship through all my travails.

Walt had created a "Heart of Gold Award" which he gave out every year and donated money from it to the event. He raised the money through his Willey World charities and the first "Heart of Gold" was awarded to me. Now, I wanted to give it to Annie Albarian.

The LLS was happy to see me doing another extravaganza, but I told them it would be a much less revenued event. The fashion show was gone. The daytime celebrities came as guests and presenters. The bulk of the show consisted of performances from Broadway shows that related to the honoree. It became sort of an homage or a roast to the honoree. Either we paid tribute to him or we mocked him. With Walt as the host, I knew much of the night would be humorous.

We kept the same format as before and added the show-only ticket to generate more revenue. During the dinner hour, the celebrities mingled with the guests. I remember Vincent Irizarry from *All My Children,* who has a beautiful voice but did not want to sing, came to support both Marj and Jennifer. Teddy Sears from *One Life To Live,* Laura Bell Bundy, Ricky Paul Golden, who is now on *All My Children,* and many others enjoyed dinner with some of their fans. Peter Hermann came to give Annie her Heart of Gold Award. Even the "Broadway Kids" performed. (They were a group of young and upcoming Broadway

Jane & Josh Duhamel

stars.) They all wore Jane Elissa denim New York City Broadway jackets.

But the one who came a little late and was new to the show and extremely popular was Josh Duhamel. He was the big new star on *All My Children* at the time, and he played Leo Dupree, who was Marj Dusay's son on the soap. I had asked Walt to tell Josh about the event and see if he would come to give Marj and Jennifer their awards. I did not know if he was coming until I saw him walk through the doorway asking for Walt. What a coup it was to have him.

Backstage, Walt and I explained to Josh a little about the event, and Meaghan Schick told her story to him. He then took some time to write what he wanted to say about both Marj and Jennifer and went into the dining room to eat his buffet dinner. When I peeked through the curtains, I saw Josh sitting at a table eating alone. I could not believe that he was not being mobbed by fans. Everyone seemed to be at their own tables talking amongst themselves. That was probably the only time Josh ate alone in a crowd. He is now a big Hollywood television and movie star married to Fergie from the Black-Eyed Peas. Then he was just Josh, the mid-western boy who had come to New York to star in a daytime drama. Things do change.

Walt did his usual fabulous job of emceeing that year, and the audience again responded positively. Billy Kay received his CMVRA and spoke about how committed he was to our event. He was such a talent—good-looking, smart, young, musically inclined, and he could even dance. His mother Lynn was very proud of him, and I thanked them both for coming. Josh spoke sincerely about learning from veterans Marj and Jennifer. He was so unassuming about himself, and both Marj and Jennifer pretended to faint when they accepted their awards. But the surprise of the night came for me when Marj and Jennifer called me to the stage. They made a speech thanking me for the award, and then both of them turned around and said they were giving their awards to me for all the work I had done. I was truly speechless. The audience applauded, but I had nothing to say. I just called to Meaghan and introduced her and said, "This girl is alive because of the work we do, so thank you all."

And we walked off together.

Gianna Paterson, the chairman of our event that year, introduced a horseracing syndicate, West Point Thoroughbreds, which proved to be a wonderful addition. She and her husband had purchased shares in some horses that were owned by the West Point syndicate, and Gianna sent invitations to that group. The syndicate owner, Terry Finley, was kind enough to offer for our live auction an opportunity to become a partner in owning a quarter share of one of their horses. I told my friend Perry at the time that this package was something I wanted to bid on. It was another lifelong passion of mine to own a racehorse and watch him run. As a very young girl, I saw the great Secretariat run and I was hooked. My brother had gotten involved with a small syndicate with some of his friends, and I saw how much he enjoyed it. This would be my opportunity. One of the busiest jockeys at that time was John Velasquez (Johnny V as he is known in racing circles). His agent was Angel Cordero, who in his time was one of the best jockeys in the world. Both Johnny and Angel came to the fundraiser that year because Johnny had heard about it and wanted to support us. His father in Puerto Rico had been diagnosed with leukemia and the cause was very close to him. I told him and his wife to call me after the benefit, and I would try and get them information about his father's specific case. One of the advantages of being involved with the LLS was that I had access to information about leukemia, and the most up-to-date advances against the disease, and access to the best doctors in the world. I knew I could help him and eventually did get him the information that he needed.

Johnny, Angel, and a few years later Mike Smith, who had just won the Kentucky Derby, were a wonderful addition to our benefits. They were also considerate and generous with their time in greeting people who came to enjoy the show.

Mark Kudish and Ron Bohmer had appeared in the *Scarlett Pimpernel* together, and Mark surprised Ron with a "roasting"

Perry Galimidi, Angel Cordero, Jane & Johnny Velasquez

rendition of a song while Ron sat on stage. It was one of the highlights of the night. Sandra Josephs, who is Ron's wife, also sang. She had played Christine in *Phantom of the Opera* for what seemed like forever, and although she is a very thin woman, she has a powerhouse of a soprano voice. The two of them, along with Rob Evan and Ron himself, made for an evening of unparalleled Broadway entertainment. I wish I had a videotape of that night, so I could hear their voices over and over again.

By the way, I did bid on that package in 2002, and I had stiff competition.

During the auction, I was usually adding to packages as donators became caught up in the moment, and I walked around with a committee member volunteer to find the people who were bidding. That year another person was bidding on the thoroughbred package. As emcee and auctioneer, Walt was the best. He could carry the audience with his jovial manner and quick repartee. His job was to get as much money as he could, but that time it was at my expense. The other bidder kept matching me. Finally, Walt asked, "Who donated this package? Can we get two?"

I thought that was a great solution, but it put pressure on

Terry Finley to give more than he promised.

He raised his hand and said, "Okay—we'll do that."

I was ecstatic. Twenty-five hundred dollars later, I had a quarter share of a horse, and my endowment fund would receive five thousand dollars between my donation and the other one. What good fortune.

I thanked Terry Finley, and Walt led us through the balance of the show. It was truly a great night and a positive revival of the fundraiser.

cs

The following spring, I was informed that the size of the Marriott gift shop would be changing. Starbucks was going to rent some space and the gift shop was losing footage. I suspected what was coming. In June of 2003, Eileen, the manager of the gift store gave us two weeks to leave our space. Even though we always paid our rent on time and people came to the store looking for us, the hotel needed the selling space for their merchandise.

It wasn't personal, just good business, but I was still concerned. I had planned to be there through the fall, probably have another event, and get through the Christmas season. January through May were usually slow months in the shop because tourists began to come to New York for the summer at the end of June. Again, I would be unexpectedly losing my source of income. I asked to stay through Christmas. The answer was no— not possible. Time to go.

I had not applied to any Holiday New York Christmas markets because I thought I would be in the gift store. By then, it was too late to send in applications. I did not know what I was going to do to replace the lost daily income. I would have to find wholesale shows to do and sign up as quickly as possible. I was not prepared—not at all.

In the Meantime
New Friends

*D*uring the years I operated my shop on 46th Street, I did meet many new people. I became friends with Lynn Kay, the mother of Billy Kay who starred in *Guiding Light* and had performed in Neil Berg's show *The Prince and the Pauper*. Through Lynn I also met Barbara Peck, whose young son Josh would go out to Hollywood to star in *Josh & Drake* for Nickelodeon. Whenever they came back to New York, we visited, and I am proud of the man Josh has become.

Mitchell Schultz, an acquaintance of Lynn Kay, came into my life, as well. He was a man with many connections in the restaurant business and ticket-selling industry, and he loved Broadway. Lynn thought he would be helpful if I wanted to put on another benefit down the road. I found him to be a great storyteller, entertaining with his visions, and also a man who had been up and down in his life as I had. He wanted to help me continue to raise money for leukemia research, and I welcomed his contributions.

I also met a wonderful person who I call the whirlwind that is Victoria Livengood. Larger then life, fascinating, beautiful, immensely talented, extraordinary voice, and fabulous fashion sense—all those adjectives describe Victoria, the Metropolitan Opera singer. A tall, long-haired, brown-eyed southern girl who could charm you in a second, Vicki discovered my art to wear through a mutual friend. She found Jane Elissa shawls, jackets, and hats that suited her personality. When she learned that I did charity benefits, she volunteered to help. It was wonderful to find someone from the opera world as her support could help us expand our potential circle of contributors. Besides, I liked her enthusiasm and we became friends.

Within a few months, Vicki had decided she wanted to sell some of our handmade items to her opera associates all over the world. We worked on putting a catalogue together, and this was a new experience for me. I had never been photographed in a marketing campaign, and Vicki wanted a picture of the two of us in the catalogue. I appreciated her judgment, and we spent many hours laying out shawls, gloves, scarves, and jewelry for the photographer. In the end, the catalogue represented Vikki's vision, and I hoped she was pleased. She now had a whole line of merchandise to sell when she did guest appearances at different opera houses around the world. She even went on to do some designing of her own.

As time went on, our paths took different directions, but we recently reconnected at the Grand Central Market. I count her influence on my thinking about how to create and promote products as enlightening, and I know she has continued to design and collect merchandise. I am proud to have helped her in that endeavor.

ଔ

I was checking email on my JaneElissa.com website one afternoon when I got this strange email. It was sent to Jane@JE.com and it read something like, "Hi, I saw your things at the Marriott when I came with my sister to New York to see a Broadway show, and I would like to order some special items for my sister and me. We would need some larger sizes than the ones you have, and I did not know if you make XLs. We would also like to know about your charity events. Perhaps we could donate things to your auction. We have many pictures of our grandfather, and perhaps, we could sign some for your charity. Thank you. Linda Ruth."

Who?

Perry was visiting, and I called him into the room to show him the email. He said, "You know who—she must be Babe Ruth's granddaughter."

"No," I said. "This must be a hoax."

I really believed it was some kind of spam and I did not want to respond. Perry said email her back and see what happens.

I was very skeptical, but I responded by saying I did not communicate well by computer, but if she would like to call me to discuss making some things for her and my charity benefits, I would be more than happy to talk with her. I gave her my business number and never expected a response.

An email came back the next day which read, "I will call you soon and am looking forward to speaking with you—Linda."

Okay—now let's see who calls. No one called for about a week. I told Perry, "See, it was a fake."

Later that day the business phone rang and Avé answered it. She told me Linda Ruth was on the phone and would like to speak with me.

I looked at her with a disdainful face and picked up the phone. "Hello—?"

"Hi, this is Linda. Thanks for giving me your number. Sorry it took so long to call, but I had to do some appearances and sign some of my grandfather's photos so I could not call before now. I absolutely love your work and would like to have you make a jacket and...."

Is this for real?

I do not remember how we finally got together, but I do remember Linda and her husband coming to my home to meet Perry and me, and spending a wonderful two hours listening to great stories about Babe Ruth. She told us his history and the intimate details of the complicated family she had come from. Babe's life was not simple, and Linda wanted to represent the family legacy in a positive way. She recognized her grandfather's flaws but also wanted to keep his wonderful achievements and his legacy alive. He was a larger than life figure and to me Linda is the same kind of person. She has his jovial manner and big heart, and she definitely resembles him. She has a great laugh and a spirit that fights for the integrity of his name.

I would be friends with Linda no matter who her grandfather was. She is one of the most honest and decent people I have ever met. She has given wonderful items to our charity benefits, come to visit me at the Marriott, and spent time with me as my friend. And most of all, she likes my work. Who would have thought I would ever meet Babe Ruth's granddaughter?

Babe Ruth's Granddaughters in JE Designs

છ

I met Sue Aitchison from the WWF (World Wrestling Federation) when I was looking for venues for British Airways. She loved my merchandise and even wore one of my shawls to an opening night party at the WWF. She was very giving to the charity and presented us with tickets to auction off at our benefits. I had no idea at that time what a phenomenon wrestling was and how valuable those tickets were.

My friend Perry's children were in love with the WWF, and he bid on a few of those packages. Sue was kind enough to give us a backstage pass on the condition that I accompanied whoever went back. She wanted to be sure there would be no behavioral problems, which she told me might happen. When Perry took his children, I had to go to the entrance while the wrestlers were performing. Because I had a pass, I was allowed to stand there and watch as they came off the ring and into the backstage area. I was trying to arrange for a "meeting time" as they had told us to come after the performance rather than before. Wrestlers came and went by me, and I had no idea who they were. I finally spoke to the liaison, and he told me which door to go to after the show and who to ask for.

When I returned to my seat, Perry's daughter was screaming, "Did you see them? Did you see the wrestlers?"

I said, "Who?"

"The Rock and Steve Austin. They walked right by you."

I had no idea who they were. I would learn later how big these stars were. Unfortunately, they did not meet those stars that visit, but they did meet Chynna and some other wrestlers. They were very happy and satisfied with the evening. I, on the other hand, made many of those trips and still did not know the exalted company I was in, but the evenings were entertaining.

 C3

Another new person I met took me in a different direction. At one of my wholesale shows, I was spotted by two representatives who wanted to sell for me. One of them, Paul Shapiro, had a showroom, and I let him keep some of my products there to show buyers when they were in town.

One day I received a jubilant phone call from him. "Jane, I have great news," he said.

"What, did you sell a thousand jackets?" I joked—*not that we could even make that many.*

"No, the buyer from QVC was walking down the hall and saw

your jacket in my window and came rushing in, saying she had to meet you and wants you to make these for QVC. You must call her immediately."

Really, and just how am I going to produce enough product to sell on QVC? We had already done private label products for Lacy Lady, the company run by Shell Kepler, who played Amy Vining on *General Hospital,* and it was a good credit, but ultimately not that profitable.

"You must call her right now. Here's her cell phone number."

I hung up the phone and thought for a moment. QVC—large quantities, TV exposure, new people, new experiences—what harm would it be to make a phone call?

"Terry Heyman speaking."

"Hi, this is Jane Elissa. I just spoke with Paul and he—

"Oh, yes," she said. "The jacket lady. I *love* your things, and I want to meet with you. Can we get together tomorrow? I go back to Pennsylvania the next day."

"Okay, where?"

"At Paul's showroom. 9:00 a.m., okay?"

"Sure, see you then."

"Please bring other things as well. I'd love to know more about you."

"Agreed—"

And so it went—we met, she loved everything, she wanted me to go to Pennsylvania and meet more people. She'd find someone to make the jackets. All I had to do was design them. I'd get a fee, a royalty, and I'd go on TV to sell them. I'd become famous, a huge success, make lots of money and retire. Everyone's dream, right? What about one of everyone's nightmares?

Some things did happen....

I designed jackets, graduated from QVC school, went on TV, made a little money, and in the middle of working on the next group for them, the administration at QVC changed. The buyers left, and they did not want to continue with my program because my price points were high, and they were successfully working with another lower price company with larger volume. *Thank you very much, but we are going in another direction.*

Next—

I remember feeling a sense of relief. I did not enjoy going on television to hawk products. The QVC goal was always to sell as many products as possible, as quickly as possible. You were supposed to talk non-stop, be perky, receive "call-ins" from interested buyers and push them to buy as much as they could. When the woman selling bras before me came out waving into the camera shrieking, "Hi, Mom," and practically jumping up and down every two minutes over the bras, I knew I was in trouble. I would look like a lead balloon after her. I told Lisa, my saleslady, "Please speak because I am generally a quiet person."

She told me, "Don't worry, your jacket is beautiful. It will sell itself." And it did. Fifteen hundred units in five minutes. A lot of money for QVC to earn and a very little bit for me as all I received at that time was a royalty. I also had to go to the studio, pay for my transportation, and my time. The only way it would have ultimately been profitable for me was to be producing tons of designs, and I did not want to do that.

I did learn, however, to be more comfortable in front of a camera and how wonderful it is to have hair and makeup done by a professional. When I saw myself on television, I looked like a movie star. I wish I could do that everyday. I also learned about manufacturing in China as an importer. QVC connected me with people to make the jackets who had factories there as well as in India. It took one year to perfect the first jacket I did because not only did I have to approve the jacket shape, I had to teach them how to translate an appliquéd Jane Elissa collage design into a laser print and sew it on the back of a jacket. All the jackets would then be the same. Even though I am no longer doing this for QVC, I have learned about printing and replication and started to apply that in my own business. I gained a great deal by taking that step.

Kathryn Falk

The twists and turns in life are so unpredictable. One year while we still had our shop, a high school friend of mine, Rita, suggested I meet a woman named Kathryn Falk, who had founded an amazing magazine—*Romantic Times*. Rita felt Kathryn would probably love my clothes and maybe her Mr. Romance could model at my benefits. Since our theme in the store had started out as a "Remembrances of Romance," I thought that she would be a wonderful person to know. We spoke on the phone, and Kathryn came to the shop with a fabulous-looking man. He was the Mr. Romance of that year, and we talked about how we could possibly work together. It was a lovely meeting. Kathryn thoroughly impressed me with her ability to see things in a forward manner. She seemed like such an accomplished person whose ideas had come to fruition. I wanted to work with her.

Unfortunately, that was the year that Ernie passed away, and Kathryn and I did not connect. Many years later we reconnected. Out of the blue, Kathryn called me to tell me that she was having a benefit to support the soldiers who were fighting overseas. She had started an organization called S.O.S. (Support Our Soldiers) and was having a mini book-signing at a downtown hotel. It was on a Saturday, and I agreed to set up a table and donate a portion of what I sold to S.O.S. I thought it would be great to see Kathryn again and feel her positive energy. I invited her to come to my

46th Street shop and pick something out for herself. She did come and purchased some things, and I donated others to give away at the fundraiser. She had such a gregarious nature that I wished I could have one-tenth of the joy she seemed to feel in meeting new people. I was still stuck in the doldrums of my life.

My friend Tracy was in-between show business jobs and offered to help me. Perry, who had a van, would drive us early in the morning to the hotel. I packed as much merchandise and display materials as I thought necessary along with jewelry that we had in our shop, and we went to the hotel loading dock. The bellman took everything up, and Perry left Tracy and I to set up. Anyone who has ever done a show for a day knows how tiring it is to unpack your merchandise, set it up to look enticing, and then five hours later pack it all up to go home. If you do not make enough money to at least cover your expenses and the cost of your help, it can be very frustrating. I was hopeful we would have a profitable day, but when I arrived, I did not see too many potential buyers.

At that time, I did not know about Kathryn's Romantic Times Convention, and I thought if this is the amount of people who come to a New York event, what would a convention be like? But I was in for a big surprise. By the afternoon people arrived, and there were authors signing books in a large ballroom. There also were soldiers on leave and a general from Walter Reed Army Medical Center who spoke about the war and the men and women who were fighting. His words were very moving, and the conversations I had with the soldiers (who seemed so young) made me realize how deeply committed they were. Many of them loved our jewelry and clothing, and I ended up either giving them some or selling things at my cost. I did sell some items to fellow vendors and attendees, but it did not seem like a money-making day. Sometimes, though, there are other things that happen while you're selling that make it worthwhile to be there.

In the afternoon, I left Tracy for a few moments to chat with Kathryn. She explained to me that the event was small because it was put together quickly and was to raise awareness about S.O.S.

Kathryn was passionate about helping the wounded, and she had visited Walter Reed hospital a number of times. She was very thankful that I had come and told me she wanted to introduce me to some of the authors who were there. We went into the ballroom and I met some romance writers, and then Kathryn introduced me to an author who was signing books for a long line of people. Her name was Barbara Taylor Bradford—one of the most popular writers in the world. We only spoke briefly because her line was long, but I was thrilled to meet her.

While I had been wandering around with Kathryn, Tracy had been chatting with some soldiers. When I returned to the table, she told me excitedly that a Mr. Bradford had stopped by and he picked out some things that his wife would like. He said she was busy in the ballroom and would come out later.

"Okay."

She said, "No, you're not getting it. Mr. Bradford is Barbara Taylor Bradford's husband. He's a producer. She's a super-famous writer, and he likes your merchandise."

I was not putting it together. He was Barbara's husband, and she was signing books, and she would be out later to look at my work—*oh*....

That day was the start of a wonderful relationship with Barbara Taylor Bradford. She bought some clothes and called me a few days later to ask when she could see me. She loved our kimono jackets. I told her where the store was located, but it seemed out of the way for her, so I ended up going to see her at her home.

Barbara is probably one of the most prolific fiction authors in the world, and her home was magnificent, but she never made me feel like I was not her equal. There I was in this giant apartment facing the river with room after room and as at home as if I were in a studio flat. Her dog joined us, and a casually dressed Barbara listened as I sat on the floor of her den and talked about my life, and she looked through my merchandise. She never tried to intimidate me or acted in any way superior. She was truly a great lady. And I remember her giving me some books and signing them—a few for me and a few for the charity.

I thanked her profusely and she said, "Thank you for making the time to come. I'll have to get some gifts for my friends next Christmas." We hugged and I left.

True to her word, she called me and asked me to come to her home in December and purchased some beautiful shawls and other things for her friends. She said, "I hope I made it worth your while to come."

"Of course." How considerate that was of her and how nice it was of her at the end of the day when I said, "You are so talented and I love your work."

For her to say, "You are very talented, and I'm proud to be wearing your things."

That made for a wonderful beginning to the Christmas season.

෴

Once I had reconnected with Kathryn, she implored me to come to the convention. She told me they had vendors there who sold merchandise, books, clothes, etc., and she thought the people who go to the convention would love my items. She said I could also tell people about the charity work, and it would give me the opportunity to break into another market. I didn't really know the "romance" market, but I had been an English teacher in an earlier life, and I loved literature, so I thought I would give this new genre a try. Kathryn said at the convention they had parties every night, and the attendees would want to buy items from us for their parties as well as for themselves.

Kathryn opened the door to these amazing conventions and I walked right in. Not only have I met terrific authors who have become clients, but I have traveled to different areas of the United States and have seen parts of the country I never expected to see. I learned about writing again, and I also started designing specific kinds of clothing for these women. I count Heather Graham, Cheryl Holt, and Linnea Sinclair as friends and clients. By starting to go to these conventions, I opened a window that had been

Kathryn Falk, Jane & Avé

closed after the demise of my shop. If I had not been willing to look through that window, I never would have found this new direction. The courage to go forward comes with the knowledge that failure, while an option, is not the end. It's just part of the process. And after the downs, the new path begins to open up with small steps. This romance connection turned out to be the beginning of the return.

After our first few *Romantic Times* conventions, I decided to give up our 46th Street store. It had been a losing proposition financially for many years, and I had been married to retailing for seventeen years. I was ready for a change. I did not want to be captive to a shop any longer. I did not know what I was going to do besides the wholesale business, but I wanted out of retail. I had started participating in a show called Art Expo and had returned to my roots of painting. I used my collage work to create painted collage-style wall-hangings. The promoters of the art expo held at the Javits Center occasionally asked artists producing unusual work to be featured on the weekend morning television shows.

Because my work was considered "forward thinking" in the art world, I was chosen. I had to be up at 4:30 a.m., go to the Javits Center, and wait to be called. As I have stated before, I am not comfortable speaking about myself, but I do not have a problem speaking about my work. I had put my heart and soul into becoming the most accomplished collage artist I could be, and I was happy to be recognized. But I thought I would be more comfortable if I had someone with me wearing Jane Elissa apparel who could speak about my art. The perfect person was Pat Sellers, who loved my clothes, my artwork, and had a gift with verbal communication. Thank goodness she agreed, and I left the burden of promoting my work to her while I was able to talk about the actual conceptualization process—the combination of fabric, paint, beads, jewels, etc.—to create a one-of-a-kind textured image on a canvas. I was proud of the work being presented. My excitement grew when I discovered that I would be following the *very* famous artist Peter Max. He had been internationally-renowned in the pop art scene, and his artwork was shown in major galleries all over the world. He actually came over to me and told me he liked my art. The woman who worked for him wanted to buy one of my pieces. Peter offered to trade my work for his—only he wanted to trade a signed reprint, and he wanted me to give him a signed original. I said, "Original for original," knowing full well that his originals sold for thousands more than mine were at the time.

Of course, he laughed and told his assistant to just buy a piece from me. It was much cheaper. Nonetheless, he had acknowledged my work, and I was standing at a TV soundstage next to him. I felt very validated as an artist.

Even though I continued to participate in the art expo and the wholesale clothing and accessory shows, I knew that I had to find another way of bringing in a steady income. The expo occurred only once a year, and the wholesale business for one-of-a-kind items was not enough to sustain me. I was at another crossroads. This time however, I did not feel sad about closing the retail shop. Being in a shop with very few retail customers became very depressing. No matter what we did on 46th street, the neighborhood business just did not happen. I joined the block association and when people asked me where I lived on 46th

Street, I said, "No, I have a store."

"Oh," everyone exclaimed. "Where?"

"Down the block, opposite the park."

The collective response was, "Oh, we've never seen you."

One woman went so far as to say she had lived on the block for twenty-five years and had not seen us.

I remembered just sighing and saying, "Well, that's why I'm here. So you can come and shop."

But no one came.

It was time to close that door. And I did.

The Road Back

The day after I closed my 46th Street shop, there was a message on my answering machine from the new manager of the Marriott gift shop. She wanted me to come in and visit.

Again? Am I going to be back with that hotel again?

The thing I had learned about business is you never close the door. Even if things are not the best, you keep the door slightly open. An account who stops buying from you for a while could come back even stronger years later. And Broadway and the theater were in my blood. How could I not find out what the manager wanted? I called the manager, Araceley, the next day and asked to talk over the phone.

"Would you like to come back and do some trunk shows?" Araceley asked. "We are always looking to add revenue, and Luz (who worked in the gift shop) suggested you might like an opportunity to work with us, again. She told me that people still ask for you and perhaps we could both benefit with a trunk show."

Well, I thought to myself, *I have been thinking of doing a charity fundraiser again, and I'd really like to be selling in the hotel when we put on our extravaganzas.* But was I up for another extravaganza? The committee had disappeared along with the list of attendees. There was no sponsor, and I did not have the same motivation as before. I was now trying to figure out how to make enough of a living to pay my mortgage.

"When are you thinking about scheduling us?"

She replied that she would look at her book and let me know. *Okay—good—no decision today.* That would give me time to plan what I should do. I just was not sure.

It took me a week to decide if I wanted to open the door to the Marriott again. I did not wish to be disappointed and do one or two trunk shows and be told they did not have any more time slots. I had my first weekend without worrying about opening a shop, and it felt wonderful to watch Sunday afternoon football and actually read a newspaper and do a crossword puzzle. I did not want to jump in—I was very torn.

I conferred with some close friends and then I spoke to Kathryn Falk. She told me about her husband's battle with a rare form of leukemia and how lucky he was to be taking a new drug that had saved his life. I was inspired by her story and convinced myself I could handle whatever happened at the Marriott. I had always loved being there and hoped things would work out well. It was a one-foot-in-front-of-the-other decision.

In case you do not know what a trunk show is, it means that a designer, artist, or manufacturer comes into a shop as a celebrity guest to bring special pieces of merchandise that are not already sold in the store. The artist or their representative stays and meets the shoppers, and this provides a personal touch to the selling. Not only will the shopper buy from the trunk show vendor, but now that they are in the store, they generally end up shopping in other areas. These shows are ways of celebrating the "shopping" experience and making it personal for the consumer. Usually the store promotes it heavily and their good clients come. With the Marriott, since business in general is transitory (mainly tourists), it really was hit or miss for everyone. Most of the time it was a hit, but it was really potluck if anyone came in and found us. Luckily, I had established somewhat of a reputation and a client base who came to New York for the theater or who always stayed at the Marriott and knew to look for us. Things were moving ahead.

℘

For the next benefit, I was able to call on some of the wonderful people who had worked with me before. Annie Albarian and Michael from Sterling Bank chaired my committee. Michael even got us a small sponsorship. We found a fabulous new room at the Marriott, which was small but intimate and overlooked Times Square. Walt agreed to come back and host, and some of my favorite Broadway singers were available: Sean McDermott, Danny Zolli, Ric Ryder, and William Michaels. In addition, Agona Hardison sang songs from the soaps.

Kristen Alderson (Starr Manning), her mother Kathy, and brother Eddie (Matthew Buchanan) from *One Life To Live* became very committed to my event. Kristen's grandfather had died of leukemia, and I have become very fond of her whole family. Bob and Loyita, who are the two most wonderful actors and friends, also agreed to attend. And Walt brought *All My Children* as well as *One Life To Live* actors to be part of the audience. Jeff Branson, James Scott, Ilene Kristen, and Terri Ivens all attended.

The event was set up with finger foods, open bar for two hours, and cabaret seating with a very informal feel to it. I wanted it that way. I told everyone, "Just think you are sitting in my living room." No fuss, no frills, just good food and great entertainment. I even set up a small Jane Elissa Boutique so if anyone wanted to buy anything, I could sell things and donate

Annie Albarian & Sean McDermott

the money to the charity. *Romantic Times Magazine* donated magazines to be given out as favors, and we held a short auction.

It was a simple, but lovely, event and it put me back into thinking I could work comfortably on small but profitable fundraisers.

I decided to do this cabaret benefit because I wanted to recognize some of the people who had helped me. Both Sean McDermott (who received the Shining Star Award) and Kristen Alderson (who received the CMVRA) deserved the spotlight.

Their commitment to helping me raise money and their friendship inspired me to continue going forward in my life. Sean, who had been in LA doing some television work, even flew into New York to perform. When I had an art opening at the Jadite Gallery in New York, Kristen came and posed for photos with my work. She wears our designs and has been featured in the magazines in our newest venture, our "Hats for Health." Anytime I have asked her to do something, she is there. I have a great admiration for the job her mother Kathy has done in raising both Kristen and Eddie in the celebrity world. They are kind, thoughtful, and considerate young people, and if they say they are going to do something, they are there. They even came to the

Kristen Alderson, Jane Elissa & Eddie Alderson

Marriott hotel to pose with Jackie Zeman, Irene Keene, Haftum (our model), and Louise Sorel (*Days of Our Lives*) wearing our hats for a photo shoot in the gift shop. I hope whenever they might need me, I can be there for them as well.

ଔ

For all the back and forth I have had with the Marriott, I have always valued the opportunity the General Manager at the hotel gave me. My loyalty to them is unflinching. I have traveled and stayed at some of the most beautiful Marriotts in the world including my favorite beach resort—The Harbor Beach Resort and Spa in Ft. Lauderdale, Florida. The employees are helpful, and I learned through my association with the gift shop that they go through a rigorous training program. The banquet managers at our events were always present and whatever problems came up were remedied. I had my committee meetings there, entertained clients for dinner, and booked rooms for people who came to my events. Although no relationship is ever perfect and problems do arise, I continue to feel a respect and admiration for their ability to create a warm and pleasant environment for their clients and hope to maintain a strong working relationship with them in the future.

An Unexpected Twist

While I was an exhibitor at an art expo, I met a lovely woman named Corine. She has a hat company, Ophelie Hats, and we formed a mutual admiration society. I have always loved hats and my mom modeled them in her youth. I also did a little of modeling at trade shows while I was in college, but in my business, we did not work on many hats. We always had berets and caps, but not much more. Corine, however, encouraged me to expand my headwear line, and I thought it might be fun to grow that business. I immediately began looking into the idea.

My friend Perry worked with a store in Brooklyn that sold a lot of close-out merchandise. The owners of the shop looked for companies that needed to sell their overstock at a low price so they could make room for new inventory. Perry's friends, Stephen and Jeff, were able to get first quality merchandise at low prices and pass that discount on to the consumer. Perry, who often sold at flea markets, worked with them to buy merchandise for his sales. One day, he called me and told me that Stephen had just gotten a fabulous deal from a top quality manufacturer, Grace Hats, and I should come take a look. He thought the hats would be perfect for me to work on. We drove to Brooklyn and to my amazement, there were boxes and boxes of simple but beautifully made hand-knit wool, acrylic, and cotton cloches in soft earth tone colors—brown, ecru beige, tan, black, loden, green, navy, wine—a treasure chest to me.

Just a bit of info—a cloche is a bell-shaped hat, worn pulled down over the head. It can provide warmth, but in the 1920's, it was decorated and worn by elegant women. For parties, it was extravagantly embellished. All I could think of was how these were like little blank canvases to me, and what I could do to them to make them look fabulous. It proved to be a magic carpet ride. I ended up buying boxes and boxes of them and discovering other shapes as well. It was the beginning of a new artistic endeavor.

I am always surprised at how creativity strikes a person if they are open to it. I have never been able to control that side of me. I do not know where these ideas come from, but I am grateful to God that they

Valarie Pettiford
Hats for Health

have not stopped. The inspiration I received from finding those boxes of hats has taken me on the road to a new business. Did I know this was coming? Did I plan this? Was I consciously looking for this? No—but subconsciously I *was* looking for something new. And I have come to believe the theory that if you open your vistas and put out your vibrations, the universe hears you. Through all the tragedies and ups and downs in my life, the universe listened to my searching—even if I did not always know exactly what I was looking for. Happy accidents changed my life. And the discovery of those hats, pointed me in a new direction once more.

CS

Corine from Ophelie Hats suggested we apply to a Holiday Market at Grand Central Terminal in New York City. I had heard of the fair, but I usually did not participate in retail shows, so I was not sure if I wanted to submit an application. This market had the finest reputation for showcasing beautifully crafted merchandise for the holidays. You had to be juried in, and I had not ever submitted slides or still photos for shows. Corine's company is based in Montreal, so she suggested I handle the paperwork, and we submit the application together. Without her persistence, I probably would not have entered, but I agreed to file the application and we were accepted. Again—a "now what" moment.

The show is set in one of the busiest locations in New York City. At Christmas time, Grand Central Terminal is packed with people coming and going from all over the world. I remember standing in Vanderbilt Hall where the fair is held and just looking up at the ceilings. The structure itself was beautiful, and I felt very small, like a speck, in an unending space. It left me a little uneasy. How was I going to present myself? There would be many vendors. Would I have equally nice things? What about the display? I would have half of a small space—four-by-four feet. Would I be able to sell enough? Did I have to be there? Could I possibly tie my sales into making some money for charity? Questions—on and on—and then I met Connie Breslin, who worked as the merchandise consultant for the Holiday Market.

"Jane, we love your hats," Connie said at our introductory meeting. "Show me what else you have."

Avé and I had brought some shawls, purses, photos of our artwork, and a small sampling of jewelry.

"Very eclectic," she said. "I knew I was going to love your things."

She was a sweetheart—full of energy with a great fashion sense. I could tell that she liked the theater because she asked me about my work with the Marriott and then proceeded to tell me about her love of Broadway. *A kindred spirit.*

"Now, Jane," she said. "We are very particular about our displays." She handed me a rules booklet and pictures of displays they approved of. "Try to make everything neat and organized. We want easy access into the space."

It reminded me of something Perry always said, "Keep it simple and customer friendly." Not such an easy task for me who always had one-of-a-kind pieces. It is hard to display items that are all different in such a small space. I was getting anxious.

"Don't worry," Connie said. "We are here to help you. See you at setup." She extended her hand as the next group of exhibitors arrived.

That first year was a true learning experience. The fair producers had very strict rules, and I learned to obey them. My sign had to be in a certain place. The display pieces could not extend past a certain point. We could not put things higher than the "pipe and drape" booth paneling. Do not make the booth look cluttered. Make sure there is sufficient light. Be there early in the morning or you will be fined. Keep the space clean (No problem for me as I dislike keeping trash around.) and do not scratch the marble floor....

Corine was better prepared than I. Her company is much larger than mine, and she always had merchandise in stock. After the first few weeks (The fair runs from Thanksgiving until Christmas.), I had run out of hats. I literally was getting four hours of sleep between pinning, sewing, beading, etc., seven days a week to fill the space. I called Avé in to help me. It was overwhelming, but I had no complaints. I met new people, sold products, and made a little money. Who cared if I had deep black circles under my eyes and dark hair roots? It was Christmas and this was our season. Things were going well.

⋘

Another invaluable contact was Laura Blaustein, the assistant general manager for Jones Lang LaSalle, which produced the fair for the Metropolitan Transit Authority. Although not as flamboyant as Connie, she too had a charming manner. She gave me guidelines on how to make the most of my time there and the best use of the selling space. I thought of Laura and Connie as the "dynamic duo" because they were always a force of positive energy. They also wanted the best for their exhibitors, and I felt they truly cared if we did well at the show. Sometimes promoters take your money and do not really worry about how successful you are because there are always new people who want your spot. But Laura, Connie, and the whole staff seemed committed to helping, encouraging, and promoting their exhibitors. I showed my work there with an enormous sense of pride.

Through that time, I was trying to balance my trunk shows at the Marriott, my private clients, and the Grand Central Fair. I felt a little guilty about taking a break from my charity work, but I needed the time to explore my burgeoning hat business. There was some publicity for us at Grand Central Station as Larry Hoff from the Channel 11 Morning Show did a spotlight there and wore my Manhattan, New York chapeau through much of the show. He remembered me from a small modeling segment we had done together ten years prior at Grand Central Station. It was fun seeing him again as he had a great sense of humor and knew how to make everyone feel at ease. I was even comfortable talking to him on television.

The biggest surprise, however, was yet to come.

I was sitting in my studio, working furiously on finishing hats (A client had ordered a black one with only black and red embroideries for Eartha Kitt, and it had to be done that day.), when the business phone rang. Dennis, who was helping us organize our work, called me in to listen to the speaker. Gail Benko was talking about a hat she had sent a friend. I picked up the phone. Although I cannot reveal the exact details of that phone call, I am enclosing a letter written by Gail about what happened....

"Jane Elissa's hats are exceptional. They cause people to stop in their tracks and exclaim, I LOVE your hat! I know firsthand because I always receive multiple compliments whenever I wear them. It all began last November when I was extremely fortunate to discover Jane Elissa's wares in her booth at the Grand Central Station Holiday Fair. I pride myself on finding unique accessories. I had never before seen such amazingly beautiful hats. I promptly bought several and sent one off to my best friend on the future President's transition team. She, in turn, received many compliments about her hat from high-ranking staffers. As a result, Jane Elissa sent hats for the future first family. I understand that she received a lovely note from the family thanking her for the extraordinary hats. You never know where you will see one of Jane Elissa's hats!"

Gail Benko

Even though I still have not met anyone from the 2008 transition team, this artistic affirmation proved to be a thrilling experience for me. My hats had reached a fresh market. I decided to use my emerging hat business with my charity work as a combined venture. That seemingly small decision to participate in the Grand Central Holiday Market became a life changing event.

The Magic of the Wind Chimes

Sitting in my studio, newspaper in hand, daydreaming of
different times.
Ave kneeling on the floor cutting yards of fabric...
Temperatures soaring, not a breeze in the air...
Suddenly there are sounds from the hall.

A rustling...
And then bells blowing in the wind...
Melodies ringing again and again...
But there is no wind.
No door bell.

Nothing is moving except the wind chimes and no one has
touched them.
Avé comes rushing into my room.
I stare at her. She is shaking. She says quietly, "He's here...."
I nod.

I had been thinking of Ernie....

Hats for Health

I took the message from the wind chimes as a sign of Ernie's approval to move forward on my next project....This first step in my new journey was the creation of "Hats for Health," a part of my business that gives a percentage of sales from the merchandise we make and sell to leukemia, cancer, AIDS research, or other charities.

Billy Freda, Louise Sorel & Dale Badway

The whimsical hats Jane Elissa Atelier has created have been very well received. Many of my clients enjoy wearing them to Broadway performances. Lisa Rosenstock, along with her daughter Debra, became Jane Elissa clients when they began attending my events. Not only do they both enjoy Broadway, but Lisa's a lupus survivor as well as a kidney transplant recipient. She has inspired me in so many ways. Her positive spirit through all that she has endured healthwise gives me hope for other people experiencing difficult times. She encouraged me to create my hats and wore them all the time. She told me she had no more room in her closet, but she would just build another one.

I made wide-brimmed hats for people like Lisa, who cannot get sun on their faces. I also am a basal cancer survivor and have to watch my exposure to the sun. My long-brimmed baseball caps are especially useful in the summer. They look like painters' caps but once we embellish them, they become little whimsical treasures. I have tried with these hats to not only make them pleasant to look at, but also to convey a message of hope for cancer patients who are going through chemotherapy and radiation. There were not enough fanciful hats on the market that spoke to people who wanted to still feel attractive and think positively while losing their hair during a grueling chemotherapy regimen. Children who are hospitalized during this process could wear the fun and colorful hats we made. I wanted to fill that space and bring a new life force in the form of bright colors, textures, etc. to these people. I continue to work toward this goal and the experience has inspired me to make bolder choices in my creative life.

Adam Lambert

*A*nother one of my inspirations for "Hats for Health" came from the *American Idol* contestant Adam Lambert. While Avé and I were watching that year, we became rabid fans of his. I think his singing voice was clearly the finest I had ever heard on the show and being the artistic person that I am, I loved his presentation. Every week, he would interpret the songs beautifully and also wear an amazing new outfit. Watching his performances inspired me to be more creative in my work.

I was disappointed that he did not win, but I was sure he would go on to great success. I did, however, design some special hats while I was watching the show. The most exciting thing though, was creating one for him. I tried to find a place to send it to him, but I had no success. Finally, I realized he would be coming to New York to appear on some of the morning shows, and it might be possible to drop it off at one of the studios. My friends in the media were unable to give me a name of a person to leave it with, so I knew I would have to go to the studio personally. Loyita told me where the entrance to *Regis and Kelly* was and suggested I wait there.

Okay, I thought, *I'll be a fan.*

I prepared a note for him and made a beautiful shawl and bag for his mother. It was a rainy day and I began to think I was being ridiculous. Maybe I could just leave it with the guard or mail it to the studio. But then I thought this might be a chance to meet him personally and tell him how inspirational he had been.

I wavered.... What to do?

Regis and Kelly were on my TV and they were introducing Adam. It was 9:30 a.m. If I grabbed a cab, I could be there by 9:50 a.m. The show would be over at 10:00 a.m. I should make it in time to see him.

Out I went.

When I arrived, there was a line of photographers on the right and autograph seekers on the left. I joined the autograph line and another fan gave me something for Adam to sign.

Finally, he came out. I saw him look at my hat, but he was surrounded by security. The guard at the door had already checked my bag, so I was cleared to give it to Adam. They took the photos first while the autograph people waited. Luckily, the security guard had taken a liking to me because there was a mob and I had been pushed to the back. When his guard said, "That's all. We have to leave," I was still at the back of the line.

The security guard came and grabbed me and said, "I promised her," and shoved me next to Adam.

He said, "Hello."

I said, "Mazel Tov," and gave him something to sign. Then I handed him the bag and told him I had made these things for him and his mother. His security people were pulling him, and I yelled, "I hope you like them," as he jumped into a black SUV and was gone.

I was shaking as I walked away. To this day, I do not know what he thought of our inspirations, but Valarie Pettiford christened the hat I wore that day the Adam Lambert hat. Meeting Adam was a landmark for me as it proved that I could put myself out there. I now felt confident enough to approach other people whom I admired.

ೞ

I have since gone on to meet David Cook and James Durbin

from *American Idol.* I also dragged Avé to wait in line for "Mike and Mike" from ESPN to sign their sports book. I even gave them hats for their wives. Mike Greenberg thanked me, but Mike Golic said, "I can't wear this. It's too small." I hope his wife likes it. The shyness and fear that still haunts me does not stop me from taking chances any longer. Seeing the courage that patients battling diseases have makes me feel stronger about appreciating every day I am healthy. Going to meet people I admire enriches my life and enables me to continue to do things for others.

I created the website "Hats for Health" because I wanted people to purchase our designs, knowing that with each sale we made a donation to charity. Kristen Alderson and Valarie Pettiford posed for some great shots in the hats. Sue Coflin, a professional photographer, took these photos, and we have just begun to build our site. Jackie Zeman has posed as well, and when we were in California at the *Romantic Times* convention, some of the stars of *Days of Our Lives* bought the hats and posed for photos. Renee Jones, Maggie Rodgers, Judi Evans, Susan Seaforth-Hayes, Bill Hayes, and my marvelous friend Louise Sorel came to support me. Even Sean McDermott posed in a Broadway hat. With all these wonderful people's support, I have begun to take a new look at my art and find a way to use it to continue to raise money for charities.

Possibilities

My "journey" as people call it is far from over. I want to continue to enrich the world with my artistic visions. I hope to work with children so that as time goes on, they can learn how to tell a story with fabric, use their talent for painting and collage, and learn that there is a way to communicate through art. There is always a thread of a story in my work, whether it is Victorian, New York related, sports themed, or my love of Broadway. It is a way of speaking without actually uttering words. I think I was able to personally hide behind that for a long time and now I might be ready to actually speak about my work. I wanted to write this to show people that anyone, even someone as shy as I was, can experience an unexpected life. Never did I dream the things that have occurred in my life. I always wanted to share my vision, but I could not have planned this road trip. When I volunteered to help at the LLS, I thought I was giving time and effort to them. The truth was I received so much more from the giving. I never wanted anything back; it just came. And I will continue to do whatever I can to fight disease and help others in their struggles. I hope my experiences will encourage others to take the baby steps that I did. Just helping a neighbor, volunteering at a hospital, mentoring an inner-city child—all that can make life more fulfilling. Whatever your passion is, follow it, believe in it—

through the travails as well as the triumphs—know you can thrive if you just open the door. I am grateful for every day, even when I am frustrated or sad or disappointed, I go on.

I wish everyone laughter, love, and the courage to take the first step. All I can say is *Good Luck*. I'm behind you.

Flash Points—Remembrances

...Having lunch with Catherine Hickland at the Marriott and talking about marriages to David Hasselhoff and Michael E. Knight. Reminiscing about men and then thinking about designing clothes together.

...Working with Frank Valentini (executive producer of One Life to Live) on Catherine's club act at the China Club and all the sound glitches we had to deal with.

...Mackenzie Philips and her ex-husband, trying to walk down the runway together. They were not really into the fashion thing. She was very unassuming and not at all showbizzy. If anything, she wanted to be just a regular person.

...Peter Hermann from Law and Order Special Victims Unit filling in for our host at the China Club cabaret without any warning. Sitting with him—me in a panic—and he really calmly saving my show.

...Kerr Smith (Dawson's Creek) & Peter Hermann walking down the runway, modeling silk kimonos with no shirt and just their underwear. Peter worried about the wind factor so we had to use static cling for protection...no glitches that day....

...Frank Grillo, Wendy Munez, and Ethan Erikson (from Guiding Light) enjoying some quiet time together at a table at our cabaret—warm and friendly people—really wanting to help out....
...A recording artist taking "The Midnight Train" right to my

sales rack in our shop....

...The then unrecognizable Hollywood director Garry Marshall *coming into my shop looking for jewelry with upturned elephant trunks and tearing bracelets apart to get the elephant charms. Just to let you know, he paid for all the bracelets and told me when he left, "I'm Gaaaary...."*

...Meeting the fan club presidents for the first time and admiring how hard they work at coordinating their events. Becoming friends with Carol Dickson and being grateful for her efforts to help me raise money for leukemia and cancer research.

...Hats off to Debbie Morris and Debbie O'Connor (One Life To Live, General Hospital, and All My Children) *for their hard work and concern for the fans and the actors. It's not easy to pull off these meetings and they are pros.*

...Walking through Central Park with Louise Sorel (Vivian on Days of Our Lives) *on a Sunday afternoon after lunch, just clowning around for photos. Friends forever....*

...Meeting "the Contessa," the ever impeccably dressed Lynn Dell Cohen from Off Broadway Boutique, always encouraging and supportive of my endeavors—New York style at its best.

...Kudo's to Scott and Barbara Siegel for the best Broadway Cabaret Town Hall Series {and for Barbara's good taste in wearing Jane Elissa's shawls.} Love those evenings.

...My first visit to the lab of my newly sponsored researcher—Erik Martinez Hackert—and bringing Rob Evan, Walt, and Rachel Galimidi, a future researcher to the hospital. A sense of pride filled me to share with them what good work we were doing.
...The awe of seeing Meaghan Schick on the runway for the first time and watching her grow into an accomplished woman.

...Rod Gilbert, David Cone, and Mel Stottlemyer talking to Perry and I at a LLS fundraiser and learning about Mel's courage in surviving multiple myeloma.

...Sitting next to Anthony Geary (Luke from General Hospital) at the bar and talking about the old days with Jackie Zeman and Genie Francis on the soap. It was like we were good buddies.

...Remembering Crystal Chappell and a very young Jordana Brewster "strutting

Jane, Lou Diamond Phillips & Meaghan Schick

their stuff" on the runway and being so committed to the charity.

...Seeing David Gregory (Ford from OLTL) sing at a Broadway Cares benefit and telling him he could be a leading man on Broadway.

Derek Jeter & Jane

...Meeting a young Derek Jeter at a leukemia sports dinner and not knowing how amazingly talented he was.

...Maria Burton coming to our Marriott shop to drop off her hand-painted sneakers to sell and no one recognizing her.

...Entertaining Dr. Gila and her mother in our shop while they purchased JE creations and eventually bonding with them as our number one fans.

...Meeting the former Commander and Chief at a private reception and thinking how different he was in person—witty, intelligent, and taller than I imagined.

...Seeing the actress Sandra James walk down Forty-third Street in her JE hat after watching her in the movie The Dictator with Sacha Baron Cohen. What a thrill to see our work on screen.

...Greeting my relatives from South Africa with my brother Joel and his wife Edie and watching their amazement at what they called our "fabulous city."

...Two friends having a delicious breakfast at Good Enough to Eat in Manhattan—Loyita Woods and I enjoying the spring weather.

...Spying David Hyde Pierce in Barnes and Noble, politely telling him "I love you," and then racing up the stairs filled with embarrassment.

...Spending time with Stephen Macht at the Broadway Cares Flea Market and talking with him about acting and his talented son Gabriel. I couldn't believe how intelligent and handsome he was.

...Learning that Avé's granddaughter Jordan was diagnosed with Acute Lymphocytic Leukemia at the age of two and knowing our research money would help her.

...Brian Gaskill contacting me to see if he could visit the children who were cancer patients in the hospital. I'll never forget how happy they were to see someone from television. We were all moved that day. Gianna Paterson, one of our committee chairpersons, made it possible and went with us.

...Also taking Ron Raines and Christine Toy Johnson to visit the children with leukemia at Presbyterian Hospital and having to go to a private place to cry. Not so much out of sadness but with hope that these children would survive.

...Running into Tom Degnan (Joey OLTL) in the Emporium supermarket on my block. You never know wh will see a star in New York.

...Working with Vancouver fashion and music student Mina and remembering how fulfilling teaching can be.

...A New York Broadway aside, watching Raul Esparza having a star turn in Leap of Faith and being mesmerized.

...Picking up the phone and hearing Dale Badway, "Mr. Broadway," singing to me the newest song from his latest production efforts—hats off to this fabulous performer.

...Watching music students, J.J., Sandy, and Michael, rehearse with Broadway performers Claybourne Elder and Melissa van der Schyff from the musical Bonnie and Clyde, and wondering which student would be the next superstar.

...Being lucky enough to see John Lloyd Young return to "Jersey Boys" with current cast member Matt Bogart—A thrilling New York night for Avé's birthday.

...Watching Sue Coflin photographing all my hats and marveling at how great everyone looks in her photos. Fabulous job, Sue!

Corey Brunish, Leslie Becker, Victor Hernandez, Mimi Bessette, Claybourne Elder, Melissa van der Schyff, Dale Badway, and Ken Lundie (kneeling)

...Bittersweet...photo op with former Mr. Romance and actor Billy Freda and pop singer Missy Modell on the roof of my apartment building—how grand! Then I remembered that not forty blocks away the World Trade Center had fallen.

...Hope for the future—sitting and looking at the Hudson River and signing a contract to design Jane Elissa luggage for Visionair.

Billy Freda & Missy Modell

...Lamenting the cancellation of two of my favorite soap operas and saying good-bye to all the New York actors. What a disappointment for the fans—including myself. Life will never be the same.

34317146R00152

Made in the USA
Charleston, SC
06 October 2014